C000259340

THE HANDOVER

DUBLIN CASTLE AND THE BRITISH WITHDRAWAL FROM IRELAND, 1922

JOHN GIBNEY   KATE O'MALLEY

Acadamh Ríoga na hÉireann
Royal Irish Academy

The Handover: Dublin Castle and the British withdrawal from Ireland, 1922

First published 2022
Royal Irish Academy, 19 Dawson Street, Dublin 2
www.ria.ie

© Royal Irish Academy and the authors

ISBN 978-1-911479-84-0 (PB)
ISBN 978-1-911479-97-0 (pdf)
ISBN 978-1-911479-98-7 (epub)

All rights reserved. The material in this publication is protected by copyright law. Except as may be permitted by law, no part of the material may be reproduced (including by storage in a retrieval system) or transmitted in any form or by any means; adapted; rented or lent without the written permission of the copyright owners or a licence permitting restricted copying in Ireland issued by the Irish Copyright Licensing Agency CLG, 63 Patrick Street, Dún Laoghaire, Co. Dublin, A96 WF25.

British Library Cataloguing in Publication Data. A CIP catalogue record for this book is available from the British Library.

Edited by Helena King
Book design by Fidelma Slattery
Index by Eileen O'Neill
Printed in Poland by L&C Printing Group

Royal Irish Academy is a member of Publishing Ireland, the Irish book publishers' association

5 4 3 2 1

Published with support from the Department of Tourism, Culture, Arts, Gaeltacht, Sport and Media under the Decade of Centenaries 2012–2023 Programme, and the Office of Public Works.

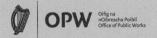

An Roinn Turasóireachta, Cultúir,
Ealaíon, Gaeltachta, Spóirt agus Meán
Department of Tourism, Culture,
Arts, Gaeltacht, Sport and Media

OPW Oifig na
nOibreacha Poiblí
Office of Public Works

A note from the publisher
We want to try to offset the environmental impacts of carbon produced during the production of our books and journals. For the production of our books this year we will plant 45 trees with Easy Treesie.

The Easy Treesie—Crann Project organises children to plant trees. Crann—'Trees for Ireland' is a membership-based, non-profit, registered charity (CHY13698) uniting people with a love of trees. It was formed in 1986 by Jan Alexander, with the aim of 'Releafing Ireland'. Its mission is to enhance the environment of Ireland through planting, promoting, protecting and increasing awareness about trees and woodlands.

Opening page: The Palace Street gate of the Castle, armoured and loopholed, with a British sentry on guard duty watching prior to the arrival of the Provisional Government, 16 January 1922. The fringe of a canvas screen to block views into the Castle is visible at the top of the picture.

CONTENTS

GLOVES
are a serious drain on every lady's Dress Allowance.

Those sent to
PRESCOTTS
regularly have the advantage of looking clean, but not cleaned.

Phone 571

EDITORIAL
TELEPHONE
104
TELEGRAMS—
"HERALD,"
DUBLIN.

EVENING

VOL. 31.   NO. 13.   DUBLIN. MONDAY,

Dublin Castle in H

THE HANDING OVER

Preparatory Arrangements at Dublin Castle

HISTORIC SCENES

Huge Crowd Witnesses the Posting of the Last Guard

Historic scenes were witnessed at Dublin Castle to-day prior to the handing over of the building to the Provisional Government of the Irish Free State.

From an early hour crowds thronged the approaches, and a vast assembly witnessed the posting of the last guard at one o'clock, the ceremony evoking considerable interest.

Promptly at 1.30 o'clock Messrs. Collins, Cosgrave, Duggan, Hogan, Lynch, McGrath, MacNeill, and O'Higgins entered Dublin Castle and at once proceeded to take over and invest themselves with all the powers of Government.

VAST ASSEMBLY

Posting of Last Guard Evokes Considerable Interest

The most historic scenes associated with Ireland for many a century are being enacted to-day at Dublin Castle.

In the course of the afternoon this gloomy building, with a sinister record going back hundreds of years, will be in the hands of the Irish nation.

From some hours before 11 o'clock this forenoon crowds thronged the approaches to the lower gates in Dame street, and watched with strained and tense vision the movement of troops, ambulances, and motors, going and coming.

AUXILIARIES ADDRESSED.

A scene of greatest about 11.30 by the arrival of a number of Auxiliaries of "Company" who were addressed on parade in Ireland just prior to disbandment.

There was a general air of breaking up about the place, and lorries laden with documents, bedding, accoutrements, etc., were constantly passing and re-passing.

In the Lower Castle Yard were groups of [...] representing the Press of the world, and there was the usual small amount of [...] It could not be [...]

THE AUXILIARIES

Official Statement From Dublin Castle

In connection with the trouble which has arisen in respect of the demobilisation of the Auxiliary Forces the following official statement was issued from Dublin Castle to-day:—

The Right Hon. Sir John Anderson, K.C.B., on behalf of the Imperial Government, accompanied by Col. Winter, C.B., C.M.G., yesterday received a deputation from the Auxiliary Division, R.I.C., to hear certain representation on the subject of the terms offered by the Government to members of the division on its disbandment. The main object of the deputation was to establish a pooling scheme outside the contract terms in order to provide for those members whose contracts with the Government have expired, and who are, therefore, worse off on dispersal than those with some months still to go.

AN UNDERTAKING.

The deputation was informed that if such a scheme could be established on a voluntary basis it would have the Government's cordial support and possibly some assistance from Imperial funds, but the Government could not possibly entertain a proposal which would upset some time [...]

MR. DE VALERA

Attitude to Treaty Explained

IMPORTANT INTERVIEW

Analysis of the Oath to be Taken

By the courtesy of the International News Service, we are enabled to publish the following interview which Mr. D. O'Connell, its staff correspondent in Dublin, has had with Mr. De Valera yesterday:—

Mr. O'Connell writes:—

To-day Mr. Eamonn de Valera received me at his home and granted the first authentic interview since opening the Anglo-Irish negotiations to me as representative of the Hearst newspapers.

For several days I sat in the Dáil session listening to Mr. De Valera and the forty-six of his supporters who spoke of an Irish Republic in motion against the ratification of the Anglo-Irish pact signed in London on December 6. Though several of these speeches were lengthy, and several delegates took the floor three or six times, there was always the ghost of the now famous document No. 2, and the equally famous oath which Deputy Milroy hauled out of the cupboard in the background, and when the session ended one was equally at a loss to understand how an oath to the British King and external association with the British Commonwealth could be consistent with an Irish Republic real.

CASE EXPLAINED.

I asked Mr. De Valera to explain his case, and he did so in the following interview:—

My first question was why he would not accept the Anglo-Irish Treaty as a stepping stone to full freedom for Ireland Mr. De Valera's reply was sharp. "Because it is not a stepping stone but a barrier in the way to complete independence," he said; "and the British Act resulting from it accepted in Ireland it will certainly be maintained that a solemn binding contract has been voluntarily entered into by the Irish people and Britain will seek to hold us to that contract.

"It will be cited against the claim for independence of every future Irish leader.

A YEAR AGO.

"A little over a year ago, when I sought official recognition from the Government of the United States, I was able to plead as a basis for Ireland's right to 'free and partial self-determination, that the people of Ireland constituted a distinct and separate nation, ethnically, historically, and as tested by every other standard of political science that they had never voluntarily accepted British rule or authority, but had consistently challenged it through the centuries, and that they had in fact by recent national plebiscites clearly indicated their will to live their national life as an Independent Sovereign State. These statements could not at that time be challenged. The circumstances surrounding the so-called Act of Union of 1800 were so notorious as [...]

MYSTER

Sensational

FATE OF

Statement A

In connection with the myst[...] of an hotel at Horsh[...] definitely ascertained [...] Hon. Victor Gibson,

The body was identified by [...] family Deceased, [...] had been away from [...] Horsham stayed at a [...]

The result of the post mo[...] from natural causes. An inquest will be held this

(Press Association Special Teleg[...]
London, M[...]

The Horsham police are endeavo[...] trace the identity of the strange m[...] was found dead in the smoke roo[...] Crown Hotel, Horsham, on Saturd[...]

Mr. Alfred Jones, the manage[...] Black Horse Hotel, Horsham, inte[...] to-day by a special representative [...] Press Association, said it was abo[...] on Friday evening last that the str[...] came in and had a drink. He ask[...] I could put him up for the night. He [...] had no luggage with him, but coul[...] substantial deposit. I said that w[...] in the circumstances, and he ga[...] pound note. I think he had other [...] his hand at the time.

DOWN AGAIN.

He was shown to his room, an[...] wards came down and asked if h[...] have something to eat. He had e[...] eggs on toast, and, as he came ou[...] coffee-room, took some silver fr[...] pocket and gave the waiter a s[...] He then went out, saying he w[...] to the pictures. Returning abo[...] he said he had not seen much of [...] he had been asleep most of the [...] had a hot rum, and told me he [...] touch of the 'flu. He then went [...] taking another hot rum with h[...] his room.

DIFFERENT NAMES.

On Saturday morning he had [...] hot rum and came down to break[...] before 10 o'clock. Having locke[...] papers he asked for his bill, and [...] him a few shillings change from [...] paid. He bought some cigarette[...] then went out.

He told me in conversation [...]

Introduction

The front page of the *Evening Herald* on 16 January 1922 informed readers 'Historic scenes were witnessed at Dublin Castle to-day prior to the handing over of the building to the Provisional Government of the Irish Free State.'

On Monday, 16 January 1922 readers of the main Dublin-based dailies were presented with the usual annual notices for January sales in the city's well-known shops. Switzers of Grafton Street had a 'great fur offer', Hickeys of North Earl Street was running a large, half-price sale of 'ladies coats and frocks', and on Baggot Street, Byrne & O'Connell's January offering was a 'special sale of underwear'. In entertainment, the annual pantomime at the Gaiety—Aladdin, in this instance—was, according to its own notice, a 'great success'. In sports, Shamrock Rovers had beaten their Dublin rivals Olympia (now defunct) 3–1 in the FAI Cup the previous Saturday, in what the *Freeman's Journal* described as 'one of the best games seen in Dublin for many years'. Fans of Leinster rugby would have seen their team defeated 11–5 in an interprovincial match at Windsor Park in Belfast the same day. Yet some sports fans had it worse than others: a Gaelic football match between Monaghan (playing away) and Derry had to be called off after ten members of the Monaghan team, who travelled by road to avoid an expected rail strike, were arrested by Northern Ireland Special Constabulary in Tyrone. Back in Dublin, cars had been stolen by armed men across the city, and even a Royal Air Force (RAF) touring car had been taken from outside the St Stephen's Green Club the previous night.

Looking further afield, readers would have learned that a new government had been appointed in France under Raymond Poincaré, and that an American journalist was detained in Paris for trying to poison his wife. Russia was gripped by famine, while Germany was presented with new arrangements for the payment of its war reparations. The sale of opium was increasing in China, with *The Irish Times* reporting that the trade was 'in Japanese hands'. A new bridge was planned for Sydney Harbour. Readers were also informed that 63 people (presumably African American, though this was not explicitly stated) had been lynched in the United States during 1921; that the Prince of Wales was met by protests as he continued his tour of India; and that there had been a spell of unusually cold weather in Britain that led to race meetings being cancelled. The unionist leader Sir Edward Carson had injured himself after a fall in London; in Dublin, the lord lieutenant, Viscount FitzAlan, had presided over an investiture at the Royal Hospital Kilmainham on Saturday afternoon; while a memorial to six men killed in the First World War was unveiled in St Andrew's Presbyterian Church in Blackrock.

The Monday papers also included large photographic spreads covering a meeting in Dublin's Mansion House the previous Saturday morning to approve the recently signed 'Articles of Agreement'—better known as the 'Anglo-Irish Treaty', or just 'the Treaty'. It had been signed less than six weeks earlier, on 6 December 1921, and, after weeks of acrimonious debate in the University College Dublin buildings on Earlsfort Terrace, it was approved by the Dáil on 7 January. The meeting in the Mansion House fulfilled the obligations of the Treaty itself, by appointing a 'Provisional Government' to implement it. Ireland, which had been part of the United Kingdom since 1801, was to become the Irish Free State, a 'dominion' within the British empire.[1]

That morning's news also touched upon an event that was yet to happen, one that, if readers were quick enough, they could witness for themselves. The *Freeman's Journal* highlighted it with a masthead that stretched across an entire page: 'Dublin Castle falls after seven centuries' siege'.[2] As of Saturday, there was a new Irish government-in-waiting; its most obvious and pressing task was to travel to Dublin Castle—the complex of buildings that embodied British rule in Ireland—and take control of the administration based there. The details of how this would happen were unclear: 'It is not known whether the formal transfer of authority will be open to the press or will be mainly a private function. In any case, it will be at most a formality.'[3] If so, it would be a formality with a particular symbolism, one that wasn't lost either on contemporaries or later observers.

What had led to the prospect of Dublin Castle being handed over to an independent Irish government of any kind was the political revolution that had taken place over the previous decade. Irish nationalist hostility to British rule under the United Kingdom had increased in the second half of the nineteenth century, but by the beginning of the twentieth century nationalist political energies were firmly behind the objective of 'Home Rule' for Ireland: a limited devolution that would see a domestic legislature in Dublin govern Ireland within the United Kingdom. In the years before the First World War the imminent prospect of Home Rule had nearly provoked a civil war between its supporters and unionists, most especially in the northern counties of Ireland, who were adamantly opposed to it. The outbreak of the First World War postponed this potential conflict, but in April 1916 more militant separatists staged a rebellion in Dublin with the aim of securing a fully independent Irish republic. The Easter Rising lasted a week and saw numerous buildings seized by the republican forces. But Dublin Castle was not one of them; the insurgents had shot dead a policeman at the gate to the Upper Yard of the Castle but occupied City Hall next door instead. The Castle was then pressed into service by the British military in its suppression of the revolt, and prisoners were held there.

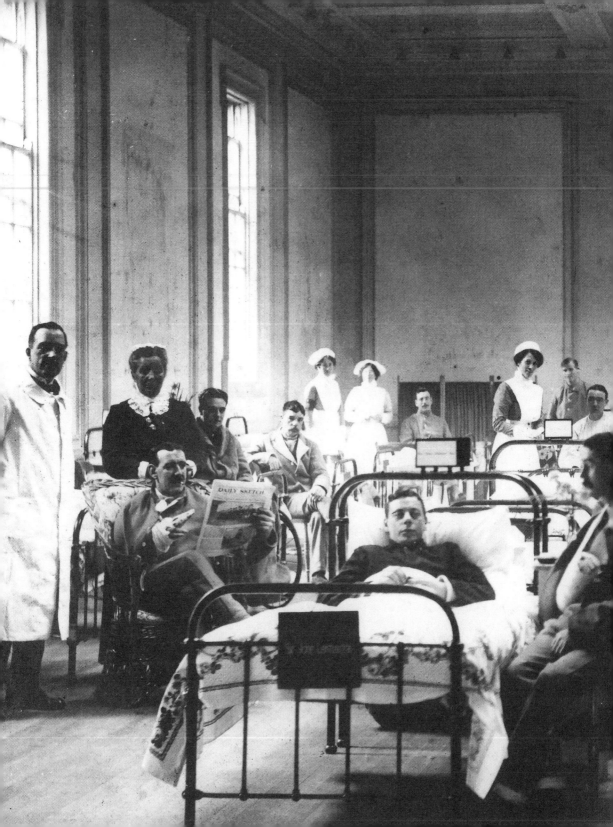

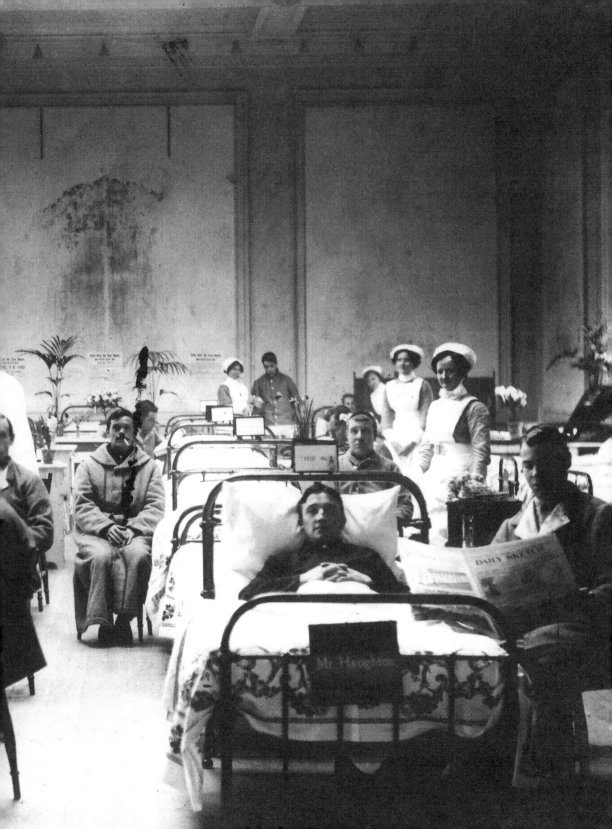

The Rising may have left the Castle unscathed—presumably, the centrepiece of British rule in Ireland was thought too large and well-defended to seize—but it transformed Ireland's wider political landscape and ultimately shifted the balance of opinion in nationalist Ireland towards separatist republicanism. One of the great ironies of Irish history is that the military defeat of the Easter Rising was transformed into a political victory for the separatists who had carried it out. The heavy-handed British response to the Rising—the execution of leaders, the mass (and often indiscriminate) detention of suspects, and the imposition of martial law—all combined to foster sympathy for the republican cause and support for the organisation that, having been blamed for the Rising, now got the credit. Sinn Féin was founded by Arthur Griffith[4] in 1905, but was officially reorganised in October 1917 under the leadership of Éamon de Valera,[5] and committed itself to the pursuit of an independent Irish republic. Alongside this came the revival of the paramilitary Irish Volunteers, the main organisation involved in the Easter Rising and which, in its aftermath, was repopulated with activists released from detention, some of whom would make an appearance in Dublin Castle on 16 January 1922. The surge in support for republicanism coincided with the decline of Ireland's Home Rule movement. In December 1918 Sinn Féin won 73 of Ireland's 105 Westminster seats in the United Kingdom-wide general election that followed the end of the First World War.

Sinn Féin MPs boycotted the parliament at Westminster, and on 21 January 1919 those newly elected representatives still at liberty assembled instead at Dublin's Mansion House and declared Ireland independent, its parliament as Dáil Éireann, and themselves as *teachtaí Dála* (TDs, deputies to the Dáil). On the same day as the Dáil met, however, in an unconnected development, two police officers escorting a cargo of gelignite in

Previous pages: Wounded soldiers recovering in Dublin Castle's State Apartments during the First World War. The Castle housed a military hospital administered by the Red Cross between 1915 and 1919.

Soloheadbeg, Co. Tipperary, were killed in an ambush by members of the Irish Volunteers. The name now increasingly being applied to the volunteers was the name by which they would thereafter come to be known: the Irish Republican Army (IRA).

The two branches of the independence movement became increasingly active throughout 1919. The Dáil devoted itself to securing support and recognition for Irish independence, and slowly but surely began to establish its own administration. Throughout 1919 the IRA embarked on an extensive but low-level campaign of attacks and raids against police forces and installations across the country. The Irish War of Independence had begun, and it intensified thereafter in a campaign of urban and rural guerrilla warfare by the IRA, followed by British reprisals and repression. A truce in July 1921 presaged exploratory talks between republicans and the British government. In October negotiations began in earnest in London, and on 6 December 1921 the Treaty was signed. The Treaty was far more substantial than what Home Rule had offered a decade earlier. But the fact that what was agreed still fell short of the fully independent republic sought by Sinn Féin and the IRA caused both organisations to split into pro- and anti-Treaty camps in early January 1922; one side would take possession of Dublin Castle later in the month.

Dublin Castle was a potent symbol of British rule in Ireland, perhaps more than any other building, so its handing over to the new Irish authorities had a clear resonance. Even during the talks that led to the Treaty, British negotiators told their Irish counterparts that 'they would hand us over Dublin Castle and withdraw their troops from the country'.[6] There was no mention of handing over anything else; the Castle took precedence, for it was shorthand for control of the country.

Ireland was one of numerous states to obtain a measure of independence in a world turned upside down by the global upheaval of the First World War and its aftermath.[7] What made Ireland distinctive is that it obtained that independence from one of the powers that had won the war, rather than emerging from the remnants of Europe's defeated empires.

BY THE LORD LIEUTENANT AND PRIVY COUNCIL IN IRELAND.

FRENCH,

WHEREAS, by Our Special Proclamation, dated the 3rd day of July, 1918, in pursuance and by virtue of the "Criminal Law and Procedure (Ireland) Act, 1887," We declared from the date thereof certain Associations in Ireland, known by the names of

THE SINN FEIN ORGANIZATION,
SINN FEIN CLUBS,
THE IRISH VOLUNTEERS,
THE CUMANN NA M-BAN, AND
THE GAELIC LEAGUE,

to be dangerous:

AND WHEREAS said Associations now exist in the County of CLARE:

NOW WE, The Lord Lieutenant-General and General Governor of Ireland, by and with the advice of the Privy Council in Ireland and by virtue of "The Criminal Law and Procedure (Ireland) Act, 1887," and of every power and authority in this behalf, do hereby by this Our Order prohibit and suppress within the said County of CLARE, the Associations named and described in the said Special Proclamation as—

THE SINN FEIN ORGANIZATION,
SINN FEIN CLUBS,
THE IRISH VOLUNTEERS,
THE CUMANN NA M-BAN, AND
THE GAELIC LEAGUE.

This Order shall be promulgated by the same being published in the Dublin Gazette.

Given at the Council Chamber, DUBLIN CASTLE,
the 13th day of August, 1919.

IAN MACPHERSON,
JAMES H. CAMPBELL.

A proclamation issued in 1919 in the name of Lord French, the incumbent viceroy, informed the inhabitants of County Clare of organisations 'dangerous to the public' whose activities were to be outlawed, specifically those 'known by the names of The Sinn Fein organization, Sinn Fein Clubs, The Irish Volunteers, The Cumann na m-Ban and the Gaelic League.' The proclamation was 'Given at the Council Chamber, Dublin Castle, the 13th day of August, 1919.' The subject-matter indicates how the rise in republican militarism was being met by increasingly repressive measures by the British.

Following the Treaty, power had to be handed over by the British, who were leaving, to the Irish. Within the British empire and evolving Commonwealth, 'transfers of power' (to paraphrase the *Freeman's Journal*) took place over a timespan that extended far beyond the origins and immediate aftermaths of the twentieth century's two world wars; British rule over most of Ireland, however, effectively ended in 1922.

Part of the objective here is to explore what happened in Dublin Castle on 16 January 1922 as a moment in the history of British empire, as well as in Ireland's struggle for independence. Ireland in 1921–2 was formally a part of the United Kingdom rather than the British empire, but aspects of the way in which it was governed, and of the institutions by which the British governed it, as well as how the British themselves viewed it, were more akin to those found elsewhere in the empire; moreover, the ways in which the British responded to the Irish revolution were shaped by their commitments to the empire, and in the post-war world more generally.[8] The question of Irish independence was intertwined with that of empire.

This short book does not offer a comprehensive overview of the administrative handover and military withdrawal by Britain that took place in Ireland throughout 1922; others have covered that territory.[9] But it will shed light on both by focusing on the event that, in symbolic terms at least, seemed to carry the greatest resonance: the 'handing over' of Dublin Castle in January 1922 to the Provisional Government established by the Treaty.

The first chapter explores the history of Dublin Castle, most particularly in terms of what it was seen to signify, and the role it played in the Irish revolution, especially the War of Independence between 1919 and 1921. The second chapter examines what happened in and around the Castle on 16 January 1922. The third chapter relates what occurred in Dublin on that date to some similar events that happened across the British empire as the twentieth century unfolded, while the fourth and final chapter explores the symbolism and public role of the Castle after the events of 16 January. The endeavour here is, through a combination of official documents, photographs and contemporary eye-witness accounts, to give a sense of the outward manifestations of power shifting at a precise moment in time and in a particular place with immense historical associations. Inevitably, there are many things this book cannot cover: its main focus is on the 26 counties that obtained a measure of independence in 1922, and it does not concern itself with partition or Northern Ireland. Equally, it prioritises one side of the Treaty divide, though some of those who eventually opposed the Treaty, and for whom the events of 16 January would have been a betrayal, naturally appear in its pages. The role of women in the revolution is touched upon, but only fleetingly, and the reactions of Ireland's minority Protestant and unionist communities to the British withdrawal remain largely outside the scope of this study. What this book does explore are some of the processes surrounding the establishment of an independent Irish state, by homing in on the moment that was at that time accorded the greatest symbolic power.

Endnotes

[1] See *Freeman's Journal*, *Irish Independent*, *The Irish Times*, all 16 January 1922.

[2] *Freeman's Journal*, 16 January 1922.

[3] *The Irish Times*, 16 January 1922.

[4] Arthur Griffith (1871–1922), writer, Irish nationalist politician and founder of the Sinn Féin political party in 1905. Led the Irish delegation at the Treaty negotiations in London and was president of Dáil Éireann (January–August 1922).

[5] Éamon de Valera (1882–1975), Irish revolutionary and later taoiseach and president of Ireland. Did not travel to London as part of the Treaty delegation and was the leader of the anti-Treaty Sinn Féin party thereafter. Founding member of the Fianna Fáil political party in 1927.

[6] Ronan Fanning, Michael Kennedy *et al.* (eds), *Documents on Irish Foreign Policy, vol. I, 1919–22* (Dublin, 1998; hereafter cited as *DIFP I*), Doc. 211, Griffith to de Valera, 4 December 1921. Accessible at www.difp.ie

[7] Robert Gerwarth and Erez Manela, 'The Great War as a global war: imperial conflict and the configuration of world order, 1911–1923', *Diplomatic History* 38 (4) (2014), 786–800; Maurice Walsh, *Bitter freedom: Ireland in a revolutionary world, 1918–1923* (London, 2015); Enda Delaney and Fearghal McGarry, 'Introduction: a global history of the Irish revolution', *Irish Historical Studies* 44 (165) (2020), 1–10.

[8] Keith Jeffery, 'The road to Asia, and the Grafton Hotel, Dublin: Ireland in the "British world"', *Irish Historical Studies* 36 (142) (November 2008), 243–56.

[9] See John McColgan, *British policy and the Irish administration, 1920–2* (London, 1983), 90–131; Alan Kinsella, '"Goodbye Dublin": the British military evacuation 1922', *Dublin Historical Record* 51 (1) (Spring, 1998), 4–24; Martin Maguire, *The civil service and the revolution in Ireland, 1912–38: 'Shaking the blood-stained hand of Mr Collins'* (Manchester, 2008), 122–69.

Chapter 1

Dublin Castle and
revolution in Ireland

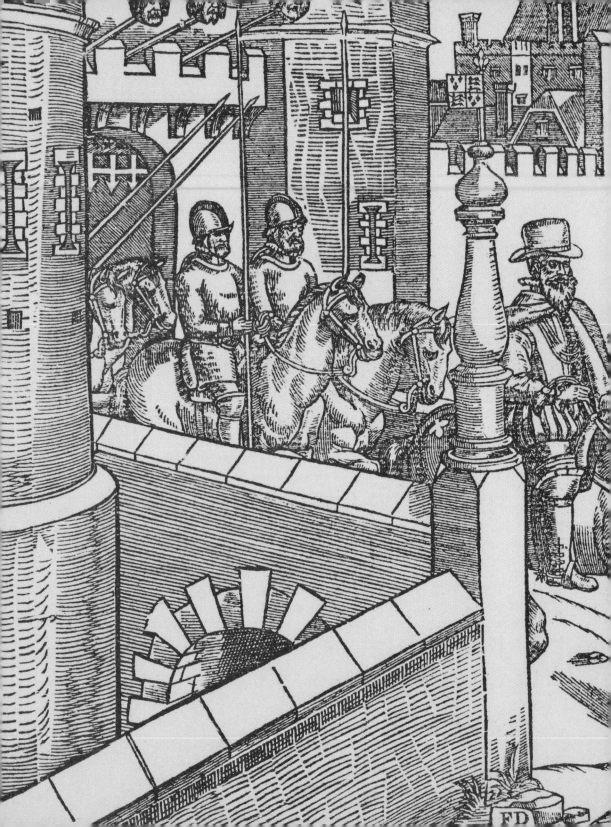

The centre and symbol of Government is Dublin Castle— that veiled, anonymous, and all-powerful institution, housed in the old fortress, which stands solidly on high ground in the heart of the capital, half-screened by a curtain of business-houses. The Castle is a world in itself, a city within the city. It is at once the Palace of the Viceroy, a military barrack, the seat of administration, and the office of the secret police... Omnipotent and omniscient, the Castle rules over Ireland.[1]

Previous pages: An early depiction of Dublin Castle can be seen in this woodcut from John Derricke's *The image of Irelande* (London, 1580), written in praise of the Tudor viceroy Sir Henry Sidney. The image depicts Sidney at the head of an English army departing from Dublin Castle; the spire of Christ Church can be seen on the top right-hand corner, with severed heads on spikes visible in the top-left.

Dublin Castle was where the British government in Ireland was based, and so the significance of what was reportedly due to take place there on 16 January 1922 would not have been lost on readers of the morning papers that day, or on those who may have heard the news called out by news vendors on the streets. Most of those who went to observe the proceedings in person, however—and there were many—had only a limited view.

For all of the prominence accorded it, Dublin Castle was largely hidden from view, obscured by the surrounding streetscape. Its location was, quite literally, at the heart of the city, which was a consequence of its antiquity.[2] As Dublin had grown over the centuries, the eastern approaches to the medieval boundaries of the city, in and around Dame Street and South Great George's Street, had evolved into lively commercial and retail districts, and the Castle lay tucked away from view within the bustling area that had been built up on what was once the edge of the old city. Dublin Castle as it existed in the early twentieth century would have been virtually unrecognisable as a medieval citadel, but its essential purpose remained the same, and gave this idiosyncratic cluster of buildings its meaning.

Herman Moll's 1714 map of Dublin City depicts Oxmantown on the north bank to Saint Stephen's Green on the south bank of the Liffey, with Dublin Castle at its centre. The location of the Castle and the circuit of the old city walls illustrate its centrality to the medieval and early modern city. The modern Upper Yard corresponds to the original enclosure, but little of the medieval fabric remains above ground.

In 1169 Welsh and English knights of Norman extraction invaded the south-east of Ireland; after the establishment of the lordship of Ireland by King Henry II in the 1170s, Ireland was under English, and later British, rule.[3] Large tracts of land, especially in the east and south, had been colonised after the original invasion, but the English colony had declined in the later middle ages and so in the sixteenth and seventeenth century Ireland was brutally reconquered and extensively recolonised, with the installation of a new, Protestant ruling elite of British extraction.[4] The kingdom of Ireland

[5]

established in 1541 was, in many ways, a colony in practice, and in 1801 Ireland's *de facto* subordination to Britain was formalised when Ireland was integrated into the United Kingdom.

One consistent feature from the middle ages to the twentieth century was that Dublin Castle served as the physical centerpiece of British rule in Ireland. A fortification had existed on the site of the Castle since the 1170s, and in 1204 King John ordered the construction of what became Dublin Castle, to secure control of the largest and most strategically important urban settlement on the island of Ireland. The Castle was located on elevated ground alongside the feature that gave Dublin its name: the *Dubh Linn*, or black pool, formed by the meeting of the rivers Liffey and Poddle. From its foundation the Castle fulfilled a myriad of official functions, but it was physically transformed beyond recognition from

King George IV's 1821 trip to Ireland was a carefully orchestrated public relations triumph. Here is an engraving, after Sir T. Hammond, of the 'Entrance of the King into his Castle of Dublin, Augt. 17th 1821', which was widely circulated. It shows a view of the Upper Yard with the royal carriage outside the entrance to the State Apartments, right, and cavalry standing on ceremony, foreground to middle ground, right to left. A stray dog appears to have wandered into the courtyard on the left.

[6]

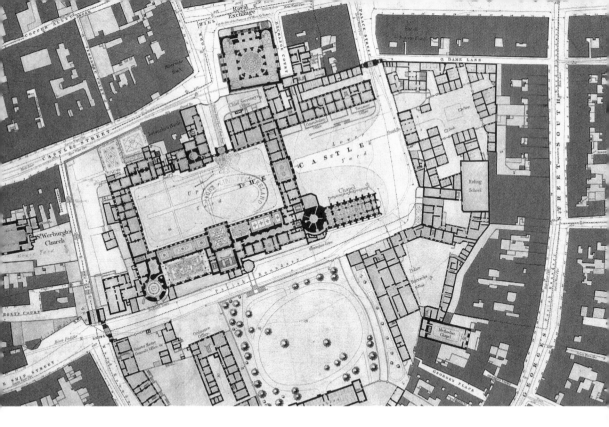

An extract from the 1847 Ordnance Survey map of Dublin showing a detailed layout of Dublin Castle.

the seventeenth century onwards. The modern Upper Yard corresponds to the original medieval structure, but relatively little of the medieval fabric remains visible above ground. In the early eighteenth century the Lower Yard took shape, extending into what were formerly gardens and stables. This period also saw the construction of the two original cross-blocks at the western and eastern end of the Upper Yard, designed by Thomas Burgh[5] and renovated later in the century (the eastern cross-block would house the Privy Council Chamber, in which, as we will see, authority was eventually handed over in 1922). The various reconstructions, renovations, additions and even removals that took place in and also around the Castle precincts in the eighteenth and nineteenth century were piecemeal rather than set-piece constructions (the Gothic Chapel Royal, completed in 1815, was a notable exception).

In the early modern era, the Castle lay at the heart of a web of official buildings in the city, including the Tholsel, Christ Church and the Parliament House on College Green. The Castle itself had evolved into a collection of buildings where power was centred, rather than being a more traditional, fortified structure that one might expect of a castle. Observers of and visitors to the Castle in later centuries seem to have been underwhelmed by its appearance. The nationalist journalist and historian Richard Barry O'Brien noted in 1909 that '*physically* it is not a castle at all…In fact, the thing is more like a barrack than a castle'.[6] Elegant as much of the Georgian reconstruction was, the aesthetics of Dublin Castle were very different from those of the more grandiose official buildings that came to exemplify and magnify British power elsewhere. It is worth noting

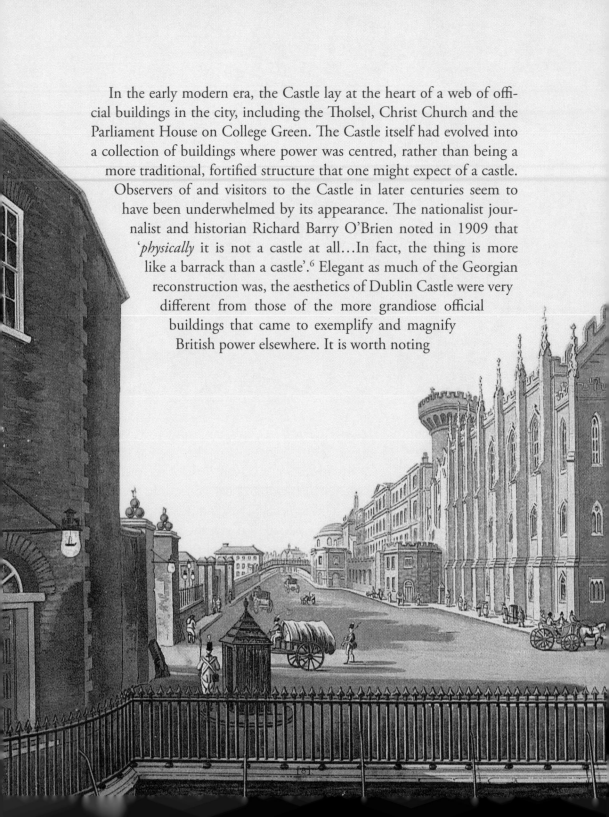

the architectural historian G.A. Bremner's comparison of Dublin Castle to precisely such a building: the vast Viceroy's House in New Delhi, completed in 1930 to a design by the celebrated architect Edwin Lutyens. For Bremner, 'In much the same way that Viceroy's House in New Delhi came to embody British imperialism in South Asia, Dublin Castle was a monument to the same idea in Ireland.'[7] There were plenty of buildings, monuments and even street names scattered throughout Dublin by the beginning of the twentieth century that reflected British rule in Ireland, but their symbolic power was overshadowed by Dublin Castle's for the simple reason that the Castle was where the British government resided; its importance did not necessarily require physical magnificence.

'View of Lower Castle Yard', by R. Havell and Sons, after T.S. Roberts, from 1816. The Chapel Royal dominates the centre, while the gate leading from the Lower Yard to Palace Street and Dame Street can be seen on the far-right.

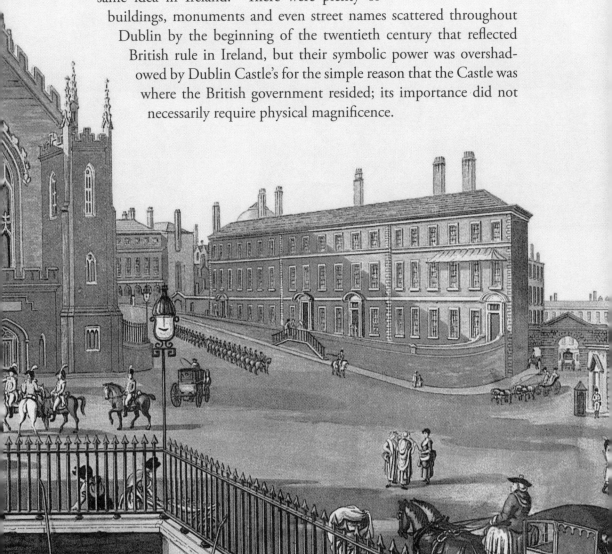

The Castle did, however, have a particular association with one individual of considerable importance: the viceroy. There had been a royal representative in Ireland since the middle ages, and the role had evolved over the centuries, as had the title. Lord lieutenant became the official term most commonly used after the restoration of

'St Patrick's Day in Ireland—Trooping the Colours before the lord lieutenant at Dublin Castle', 1880. Ceremonial events in the Castle often involved the military.

the monarchy in 1660—an event that was presaged by military officers who had turned against the parliamentarian regime seizing control of Dublin Castle in December 1659.[8] Those who held the post thereafter were aristocrats, and almost always members of what was, until 1869, the

THE GRAPHIC

AN ILLUSTRATED WEEKLY NEWSPAPER

No. 1,107.—Vol. XLIII.
Registered as a Newspaper

SATURDAY, FEBRUARY 14, 1891

WITH TWO SUPPLEMENTS

Price Sixpence
By Post 6½d.

A DRAWING-ROOM AT DUBLIN CASTLE—THE LORD LIEUTENANT KISSING A DÉBUTANTE

DRAWN BY WILLIAM SMALL

established, Anglican, Church of Ireland. The role of lord lieutenant incorporated both symbolism and substance, and the informal designation 'viceroy' reflected the ceremonial elements of the role as the representative of the Crown in Ireland; the term 'vicereine' was applied to their spouses.

Dublin Castle had been a viceregal residence since the 1560s, but viceroys were generally absentees from Ireland until the latter decades of the eighteenth century. The Georgian remodelling of Dublin Castle was not done on the basis that the viceroy would automatically be living there (the Viceregal Lodge in the Phoenix Park became an official residence from the later eighteenth century).[9] Yet as viceroys became more permanent residents in Ireland, the ritual dimensions of the role became more prominent. It was a unique, if not anomalous, role within the United Kingdom after 1801 and was likened by critics to that of a colonial governor; the Irish post inspired elements of the equivalent position later established in India.[10]

The prestige accorded by the presence of the viceroy gave rise to another dimension of life in the Castle, and within the orbit of its walls: the social scene that existed around the viceregal court, with its annual round of balls and entertainment, all hosted in the Castle's lavish rooms. Such scenes were vividly evoked in George Moore's[11] 1886 novel *A drama in muslin*, depicting an 'effluent tide of satin and silk discharging itself into St Patrick's Hall'.[12] These events were largely the preserve of Dublin (and Ireland's) upper classes, both Protestant and, increasingly in the Victorian era, Catholic. The pejorative term 'Castle Catholic' was often applied to those Catholics who were seen aligning

Previous page: Cover image from *The Graphic*, 14 February 1891, Valentine's Day, depicting 'A drawing-room at Dublin Castle - the Lord Lieutenant kissing a débutante'. The Dublin season kept both viceroy and vicereine occupied from January to March with dinners and receptions. The season culminated with the annual St Patrick's Day ball, held at the Castle on 17 March in the splendid mirror-lined hall that bears St Patrick's name.

Opposite: 'The Royal Visit to Ireland', from *The Illustrated London News*, 18 April 1885. A depiction of a ball in St Patrick's Hall on the occasion of the visit to Ireland of Albert Edward, Prince of Wales (the future King Edward VII), and Alexandra, Princess of Wales.

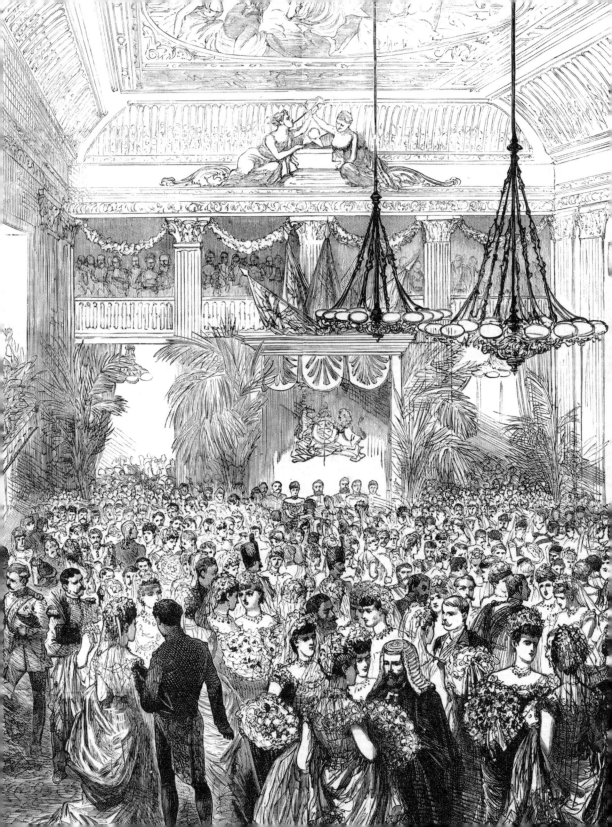

themselves with the British regime, socially and politically.[13] That said, the prestige of the office of the Irish viceroy diminished throughout the nineteenth century; by the early twentieth century the chief secretary (the minister in charge of Irish affairs) had evolved to become the key figure in the Irish administration.[14] The role of the aristocratic viceroy had been eclipsed by the more ordinary administrator.

Dublin Castle was where the levers of power in Ireland lay. All political, security and financial policies evolved there. While the organs of the British administration were scattered across a variety of locations in Dublin, the distinctive cachet of the Castle arose from the fact that the principal offices were located within its walls. Richard Barry O'Brien succinctly captured this point in 1909: '*politically*, the Castle is the Executive, and the Executive consists of the Lord-Lieutenant, the Chief Secretary and the Under-Secretary', the latter being the deputy to the chief secretary.[15] Next in the Castle hierarchy came the chief legal officers and the heads of the government departments. Security policy too was shaped in the Castle: it housed the commissioner of the Dublin Metropolitan Police (DMP), the inspector-general of the Royal Irish Constabulary (RIC) and the prison board. Alongside these were branches of central administration such as the treasury and financial offices, with a host of other official bodies close by. The significance accorded to Dublin Castle arose because decisions were made there.

The complexion of the Irish administration had, to some degree, started to shift away from a traditional reliance on the Protestant landed and professional classes in the generation prior to the Irish revolution. Nevertheless, on the eve of the First World War, the upper echelons of the Irish civil service and police forces were still disproportionately

A postcard from the revolutionary era, with Christmas greetings in Irish, marking the famous escape of the Irish chieftain Red Hugh O'Donnell (Aodh Ruadh Ó Domhnaill) from Dublin Castle, Christmas 1591. The image is sanitised; he escaped by shimmying down an open latrine on a silk rope. The symbolism of his escape from the clutches of English power had an enduring popularity to later generations of nationalists, often being mentioned in discussions of the history of the Castle.

Nodlaig na Saoirse duit.

Escape of RED HUGH. Christmas Eve. FROM DUBLIN CASTLE

Fagan

Nº 1612

Protestant; the proportion of Catholics in senior positions had increased, but they were often drawn from the landed and professional elites and, like their Protestant counterparts, could be classed as broadly unionist in their politics.[16] There had been change, but not necessarily at the top. Even before the revolution, in 1907, Augustine Birrell,[17] the recently appointed chief secretary for Ireland, spoke in Westminster of

> a system which is called, more conveniently than accurately, Dublin Castle…it is, to use a familiar expression, 'switched off' from the current of national life and feeling; and one cannot feel—I do not believe anybody within the walls of Dublin Castle can feel—that that is the way to secure the regeneration of Ireland.[18]

A list of some of the government departments based in Dublin Castle under the British regime prior to 1922.

Opposite: Two RIC officers on duty at the entrance to Dublin Castle, *c.* 1920–1. A sleeping dog lies on the footpath to their right.

Any reply should be addressed to :—

THE UNDER SECRETARY,
DUBLIN CASTLE.

...lowing number quoted :—

CHIEF SECRETARY'S OFFICE,

DUBLIN CASTLE.

Departments under British Administration.

LIST OF GOVERNMENT DEPARTMENTS IN IRELAND

WITH ADDRESSES TO WHICH CIRCULARS SHOULD BE SENT.

(A) DEPARTMENTS OF THE IRISH GOVERNMENT.

(1).   The Secretary,
Department of Agriculture & Technical Instruction,
Upper Merrion Street, Dublin.

(2).   The Secretary,
Agricultural Wages Board,
14, Stephen's Green, Dublin.

(3).   The Secretaries,
Commissioners of Charitable Donations and Bequests,
2, Kildare Place, Dublin.

(4).   The Assistant Under Secretary,
Chief Secretary's Office,
Scottish Provident Buildings, Belfast.

(5).   The Chief of Police,
Dublin Castle.

(6).   The Chief Crown Solicitor,
Dublin Castle.

(7).   The Secretary,
Congested Districts Board,
Rutland Square, Dublin.

(8).   The Chief Commissioner,
Dublin Metropolitan Police,
Dublin Castle.

(9).   The Chief Magistrate,
Dublin Metropolitan Police Courts,
Inn's Quay, Dublin.

(10).   The Secretaries,
Office of National Education,
Marlborough Street, Dublin.

(11).   The Assistant Commissioners of Intermediate Education,
1, Hume Street, Dublin.

(12).   The Secretary,
Endowed Schools Commission,
33, Stephen's Green, Dublin.

(13).   The Secretary,
General Prisons Board,
Dublin Castle.

Fifteen years after Birrell made his observations in Westminster, George C. Duggan,[19] who served in a senior role in the chief secretary's office, expressed similar sentiments when describing Sir John Taylor,[20] the incumbent assistant under-secretary, as the last of those who

> to the Ireland without, typified 'Dublin Castle' for all time—a machine, a car of Juggernaut that crushed its victims beneath its wheels, while in the temple within the lordly priests and the temple maidens—fair and sometimes frail, if the whispers of Dublin Society for the last hundred years are to be believed—made a jest of life.[21]

If these were views from inside the Castle, the view from the outside could be very different. Kevin O'Shiel,[22] recalling the pre-war Dublin of his student days, described the multi-faceted city of his youth and in so doing gives us an account of the culture and norms that apparently surrounded the Castle regime:

> Apart from the Dublin of studentdom, there were, in those days, at least half a dozen different Dublins, each living its own self-contained life, and having greater or lesser contacts with the other Dublins.
>
> There was, first of all, Castle Dublin—the official Dublin of the British Raj, headed by the Lord Lieutenant, and comprising the officers of the army of occupation, the heads of the Civil Service quartered in the Castle, and in various Government Departments, scattered throughout the city; the heads of the RIC and DMP; the law officers of the Crown, and the Judges of the Court of Appeal and the High Court. These constituted a ruling caste, a separate section of society, living an Olympian and largely exclusive existence in the midst of the commonalty, meeting in exclusive clubs such

as the Kildare St., the Sackville and the Hibernian United Services Club. They were, such of them as were permanent, nearly all strong Unionists of a definitely Orange tinge, many of them English, particularly in the higher ranks, with little or no real sympathy for the people or their aspirations. It is true that when the Liberal Government came into power, the political chiefs then appointed, such as the Earl (later Marquis) of Aberdeen and Augustine Birrell, his Chief Secretary, were avowedly sympathetic with Irish Nationalism in its Home Rule form; but the permanent chiefs of the Castle Civil Service, never changed on a change of government, remained *'semper idem'* adamantly hostile to Irish nationalism, even in its feeblest form, and avowed protagonists of the Union, which they regarded as being synonymous with loyalty.[23]

Here was an unflattering representation of a world that O'Shiel, as an official of the incoming Irish Free State in 1922, would help bring to an end. Eamon Broy[24] of the DMP, by providing information to the IRA during the War of Independence, could be said to have done likewise. He summed up the Castle in a blunt fashion: 'Dublin Castle' he recalled, was 'believed by the people to be the centre and focus of all that was evil and secret and sinister.'[25]

The point was not just applied to British rule in Ireland. In Egypt too, Irish nationalists saw parallels with revolutionary activity and its repression there. One report in the Westmeath press on the activities of the colonial secretary, Lord Milner,[26] in Egypt (where he was heading a commission investigating the prospect of conceding some form of self-government) described him as issuing forth from 'the Dublin Castle in Cairo'.[27] The term had become a shorthand for British rule over unwilling subjects. The headlines of the Dublin dailies that followed the handing over of the Castle in January 1922 were of a similar tenor. For the *Irish Independent*, this 'Site of evil rule passes into the nation's

control', and the *Freeman's Journal* exclaimed that the 'Surrender of Sinister Symbol of Alien Rule [was] Received'. There was little scope for ambiguity.

By the end of 1919 the British coalition government of David Lloyd George[28] had recognised that a withdrawal from Ireland's domestic affairs was a political necessity if there were to be a settlement of the 'Irish question'.[29] A necessary prelude was the reform and restructuring of the government based within Dublin Castle. In May 1920 Sir Warren Fisher,[30] the secretary of the Treasury, subjected the Castle regime to a scathing critique. There was some acknowledgement that the Castle had often simply picked up the pieces left by decisions made in isolation in London.[31] But Fisher bemoaned the hard-line political stance of the Dublin Castle administration and its

Republican separatism was on the march in the years after 1916 and the British had sought to stifle this new militancy from an early stage. May 1918 saw the appointment of a viceroy, Sir John French, Viscount French of Ypres, pictured here in the Council Chamber of Dublin Castle soon after taking up his posting. Note the top hats.

Members of F Company of the Auxiliary Division of the RIC, photographed in uniform with the Chapel Royal in the background, *c.* 1920. Recruitment for this paramilitary unit began in July 1920, and these new forces acquired an unenviable reputation for brutality and indiscipline after they were deployed as the British administration in Ireland stepped up its campaign against the IRA. The photograph is from the papers of Piaras Béaslaí, who was a publicity officer for the Dáil government and the editor of the IRA newspaper *An tÓglach*. It appears to have been annotated, possibly to identify those pictured.

alignment with the 'ascendancy', and effectively recommended a purge of the key positions in a government that he characterised as 'almost woodenly stupid and quite devoid of imagination'.[32] A raft of new appointments followed, along with a distinct change in policy and approach. This was undertaken as the prelude to a settlement, however, and the Castle's reputation was almost certainly beyond redemption in the eyes of nationalist Ireland. As Duggan put it, more bluntly, government policy in Ireland was 'always damned under the title "Dublin Castle"'.[33]

The British government recognised the need for a political settlement in Ireland but was also committed to attempting to crush the independence movement. The Irish War of Independence intensified in scale and scope throughout 1920 and Dublin Castle became increasingly fortified as the conflict unfolded. Three companies of the newly recruited auxiliary cadets (a paramilitary adjunct to the RIC) were based there. One of them, F Company, actively participated in raids around the city. In August 1920 many officials and civil servants, including those seconded from England and who had previously been ensconced in the Marine Hotel in Dún Laoghaire (Kingstown), relocated to the safer confines of Dublin Castle.[34] The Mayo-born revolutionary Ernie O'Malley[35] noted how, by autumn 1920 the Castle 'was again a fortress which higher officials seldom left openly'.[36] For security reasons, even Sir John Anderson[37] and his colleagues in the Irish administration were advised to live within the cramped confines of Dublin Castle, where their offices were situated. Anderson took up riding for exercise, unperturbed in the face of the threat of assassination by the IRA, but others were soon targeted.[38]

The most notorious events of the conflict in Dublin came on Bloody Sunday, 21 November 1920, when the IRA killed a large number of British officers (along with some civilians) at their lodgings around Dublin. It was a watershed in the conflict; its immediate consequence was a British attack on a crowd attending a football match at Croke Park, in which fourteen (mostly civilians) were killed. Concerns over the implications of the IRA attacks prompted even more officials and security personnel to relocate to the Castle. A number of adjacent buildings, which had been requisitioned as buffers to protect the Castle from attacks, were now pressed into service as accommodation. In January 1921 the buildings at 3 and 4 Palace Street, near the entrance to the Lower Yard of the Castle, were commandeered as being 'dangerous houses'.[39] Overcrowding led to a ban on wives moving in, though some were enrolled as typists to get around this stricture and were apparently accommodated on Palace Street. Some families also now lived inside Dublin Castle itself, where the children led, according to Duggan's recollections of the hustle and bustle within, 'an Arcadian existence, without lessons, without governesses'.[40] If this were true for children, it was certainly not the case for the adults. The ongoing confinement of people within the complex led to tennis courts being laid out in the walled garden behind the state apartments, which permitted some degree of exercise and entertainment. Eamon Broy recalled how DMP commissioner Walter Edgeworth Johnstone[41] was accustomed to walking in and out to the Castle from his home in Booterstown until 'it dawned on him in early 1920 that this was no longer a healthy habit'. He moved into the Castle, where he and other senior officers now tried their best to exercise, in dispirited fashion, 'inside the comparative safety of the lower Castle yard'.[42]

The exterior of the Castle, insofar as it could be seen, told its own story about the conflict. The lower gate and its adjacent buildings were draped with barbed wire and mesh to prevent bomb attacks. There was even barbed wire placed inside the culvert for the River Poddle, regularly checked by Royal Engineers. Sentries and machine-gun posts were placed on some of the more exposed rooftops such as on the Record Tower, where the union flag usually flew. Canvas screens were erected inside and around the complex to prevent the movements of people and vehicles from being seen from nearby rooftops. The gate to the Upper Yard, beside City Hall on Cork Hill, was closed, while the lower gate on Palace Street was guarded by military police and members of the DMP, who could draw upon the services of the auxiliaries as required. The Lower Yard was used as parking for military vehicles, and Patrick Moylett,[43] who was acting as an intermediary between the independence movement and the British as they moved towards negotiations, recalled auxiliaries outside the Chapel Royal in May 1921 'firing revolver shots at small barrels filled with clay, the class of barrels that came from Spain with grapes'.[44] David Neligan[45] also left a vivid account of the Castle at the height of the conflict, when it was 'virtually in a state of siege':

All night long the Square gleamed with headlights as raiding parties came and went. Officers and civilians dashed in and out in covered cars. About 100 Auxiliaries were quartered there—the notorious F Company. They were an extraordinary collection. I saw men in Airmen's uniforms, highlanders complete in kilt, Naval officers, Cowboys and types from every quarter of the globe. A sprinkling of the crowd wore the blue tunics of the R.I.C. with the letters 'T.C.' (temporary cadets). All wore glengarry caps. Some wore old British Army uniforms. Auxiliaries were paid £7 (seven pounds) a week, most of which went to the Canteen, which did a roaring trade, night and day. Once, when cash ran out, a squad raided the City Hall in broad daylight and stole several thousand pounds. Night after night a dark tall fellow wearing a Colonel's epaulettes and a glengarry cap was frog-marched to a lorry by his men. I did not know his name. Some of them, including the S.S. [secret service] men, adopted a different name for every day of the week. He was so drunk that he could not proceed under his own steam but at the same time insisted on going out to look for the 'Damn Shinners'. He was left in the front seat of an open Crossley tender, a pair of which always travelled together.[46]

The IRA carried out many attacks in central Dublin throughout the War of Independence, but Neligan was quite scathing of the fact that 'from the beginning to the end one serious attack was not launched on the Castle auxiliaries'.[47] Likewise, according to Eamon Broy, Michael Collins[48] 'had plans all the time for burning or blowing up portions of Dublin Castle … However, nothing ever happened afterwards in this line'.[49]

What the IRA could and did do was obtain useful information from within the Castle from individuals working there, from sympathetic eb.

1920. Was instructed to get in touch with a Mr. Bob. Collins who was
engaged in a Canteen in the Castle, with a view to procuring
information as to movements of British Forces.
Contact was made with Mr. Collins and he agreed to pass on to me
any information that he would pick up in the course of his contact
with Auxiliaries and British Military in the Castle. We arranged
a meeting place at a house in St. Albans Road, S.C.Rd. where I met
Mr. Collins at various hours of the day and night and collected
what information he had, this was taken to my home on Rathmines
Road, typed out and passed on to Miss Moira O'Byrne who was the
direct line with the D/I Miceal Collins. The information received
concerned the names of prisoners recently lodged in the Castle,
where they came from and the charge against them, this was passed
on to the D/I who in turn made contact with the Prisoners through
me. Details of Auxiliaries, Company strength, information as to
raids for wanted men, when such information came through it had to
be taken to Miss O'Byrne at all hours to her home at Highfield Rd.
for trasmission to the D/I. Information as to alarm switches
that had been installed for the purpose of notifying any attacks
on the Castle, (details of which had been given to Supervisors
only) this information was passed on to my brother J.J.Brennan
who was attached to the I.R.A Headquarters Intelligence, special
Telegraphs section. I was engaged all the time on this type of
work and had very little contact with others engaged on work of
National importance as I was instructed to make sure my contact
with the Castle was not broken or suspected by attending parades.
During 1921 this work grew larger and it was common to remain up
most of the night preparing reports, receiving reports and rushing
same to Highfield Road for the D/I. I kept arms for wanted men
during this period and procured safe houses for men from the
country in town for business with the D/I and Q.M.G. My contact
with the Castle kept me busy all the time as it was a wholetime
job and I had to be ready move any moment on the receipt of
messages that were of utmost importance to G.H.Q.

An extract from the Military Service Pension file of Annie Mary Smith (née Brennan),
describing how contact was established with a potential informant working in a canteen in
Dublin Castle, 'with a view to procuring information as to movements of British Forces'.

A studio portrait of Lily Mernin and her cousin, Piaras Béaslaí. She was employed as a short-hand typist at the garrison adjutants' office in Dublin Castle. Mernin was introduced to Michael Collins by Béaslaí and began work as an intelligence agent for Collins in 1919. She became one of his most important contacts in Dublin Castle and was known by the alias 'Little Gentleman'. Her most significant role was identifying the residences of British intelligence agents later killed by Collins's squad on Bloody Sunday (21 November 1920).

policemen like Broy and Neligan, and staff members like the typist Lily Mernin, who, among other things, supplied the details of many of those killed on Bloody Sunday. Such information generally related to security matters; it proved virtually impossible for the IRA to obtain intelligence from within the Castle administration itself.[50]

During the war the Castle was used for the temporary detention of suspects before their transfer to prison; City Hall, located beside the Castle, had been seized by the British army in December 1920 and was used to host courts martial.[51] Detention in the Castle could often involve brutal treatment at the hands of the army and police, as the young IRA volunteer C.S. (Todd) Andrews observed.[52] Having been picked up near O'Connell Street Andrews, who gave his captors a false name, was taken to what it appears was the guard room in Dublin Castle, adjacent to Exchange Court. He was regularly marched through the Castle to exercise outside Ship Street Barracks, in what he felt were effectively 'identification parades'. After a few days Andrews was eventually brought for questioning in the State Apartments, where he noted the incongruous presence of a vase of daffodils ('except for the Auxiliary in the background and the daffodils, the scene might well have been an interview in the public service'). Andrews was treated reasonably well, partly as he successfully convinced his interrogators that he was in Sinn Féin but not the IRA. After being returned to detention in the Castle he briefly encountered a prisoner who had been badly beaten in custody following an IRA ambush on Brunswick (now Pearse) Street. It disabused him of the notion that British regular forces were less likely to mistreat prisoners than their paramilitary counterparts. Andrews was soon transferred to Arbour Hill: 'I was delighted to get out of the Castle'.[53]

Others were less fortunate. Ernie O'Malley recalled friendly encounters with auxiliaries while imprisoned in Dublin Castle at Christmas 1920, but he also left a vivid account of his torture there. His recollection of his detention was, in later life, intertwined with a sense of the Castle's history; he described the place as 'the symbol of all that was hateful in the British domination of Ireland' as well as 'the great symbol of misgovernment in the people's minds'. His own treatment, in his reading of his life, placed him in a long line of those who had suffered at the hands of the regimes based in the Castle.[54] But O'Malley lived to tell his tale; others did not. On the night of Bloody Sunday, 21 November 1920, having been picked up the night before, Peadar Clancy and Dick McKee, both senior members of the IRA's Dublin Brigade, along with a civilian, Conor Clune, were apparently tortured in the Castle before being killed; the official story was that they were killed while trying to escape. Eoin MacNeill[55]—later a member of the Provisional

1   2
upts   Murphy

Freeman

3 Major Price   5
4 Col Johnstone   Barrett
                   Asst Comms.

Government that would assume power at the Castle in January 1922—was subsequently detained in the 'murder room' of the Castle, and was shown a 'mark on the side of the wall' by one of his captors, who said 'Do you know what that is? That's the brains of some of your lot'.[56] Such incidents magnified the sinister reputation the Castle had in the eyes of republicans and nationalists.

Dublin Castle during the War of Independence was an intense, claustrophobic environment. Some limited social and musical events did take place there during that time, mainly for the benefit of its overwhelmingly British residents. Any potential perception of insensitivity in holding such events was outweighed by

An IRA intelligence photograph featuring a line of men, women, children and soldiers, standing in the Upper Castle Yard in 1921. Note the secure gate leading out to Cork Hill, which remained closed for much of the War of Independence. The photograph would have been used by the IRA to identify key figures of interest to them. Those identified are: Superintendents Freeman and Murphy, Major Price, Col. Johnstone, Barrett (Asst Comms), Gibson (G. Divn), Rutherford (G. Divn), Nixon (G. Divn), and Cassmaker (auxiliary). The families were presumably those of officials who had relocated to the Castle precincts during the conflict.

the need to let off some steam in the course of a lengthy confinement. Of course, social events also 'enabled the remnants of Dublin society to invade the Castle precincts in the afternoon and while away the official hours by jazz or foxtrot'.[57] In January 1921 there was much consternation when F Company of the auxiliaries tried to take advantage of the absence of some senior officers by staging a New Year's Eve ball in St Patrick's Hall and were found selling tickets for the event. An exasperated Mark Sturgis[58] noted that most of those who worked and now lived in the Castle had to adhere to rigorous security checks,

> yet these beauties can almost without by your leave or with your leave import a pack of women of whom nobody with the possible exception of themselves knows anything at all. Interesting to see when I get back to-morrow whether the Shinns have got in disguised as buxom wenches or whether failing this the whole place has been fired up by the festive ex-officers themselves.[59]

Nor was this an isolated incident. According to Lily Mernin, 'the Auxiliaries also organised smoking concerts and whist drives in the Lower Castle Yard', and some of them saw their female visitors to the tram afterwards, only to be shadowed by IRA members seeking to identify them.[60] Security in and around the Castle intensified as the conflict dragged on, but the IRA tried to exploit any vulnerabilities. G.C. Duggan, for example, left a mordant observation on the photographic identification that was introduced to get in and out of the Castle. This was 'admirably suited to London offices in wartime', but in Ireland such documents were 'a menace to those labelled in this way'; he blamed them for the death of at least one officer, and photographs were ultimately abandoned. They were replaced by the memory and discretion of the Castle guard. The threatening

A cartoon by David Low that appeared in *The Star* on 23 November 1920, just after Bloody Sunday. Its title captures the public awareness surrounding the British policy of reprisals in Ireland and the role played by the Castle: 'The Vicious Circle—suggested design for frieze for Dublin Castle.'

atmosphere in the streets around the Castle, and the city at large, weighed upon some of those who worked there. Duggan recalled that

> as one left the Castle one had a feeling of watchfulness. As I walked up Dame Street I have at times looked back with that—sub-conscious sense of being followed—and by whom? The life of a Civil Servant in London seemed hum-drum when compared with this brooding sense of fatality, but I don't suppose many English Civil Servants would have wished to exchange places.[61]

The air of menace felt in Dublin on the part of officialdom dissipated with the truce of July 1921. Afterwards, officials and civil servants began to venture out once more. The Castle remained under guard, though Duggan noted that the canvas screens in the Lower Castle Yard 'were allowed to fall into disrepair, and hung for many months in unsightly remnants'. In the meantime,

Any reply should be addressed to:—

THE UNDER SECRETARY,
DUBLIN CASTLE,

and the following number quoted:—

CHIEF SECRETARY'S OFFICE,

DUBLIN CASTLE.

19/2/21

Sir,

     I am directed by the Lord Lieutenant to acknowledge the receipt of your letter of the 18th instant forwarding further Petition on behalf of Thomas Whelan, and to say that it shall receive his most careful consideration.

     I am,

        Sir,

         Your obedient Servant,

Michael Noyk, Esq., L.L.B.,
   12, College Green,
     Dublin.

A letter on Dublin Castle stationery from Alfred Cope, the assistant under secretary, to Michael Noyk, lawyer and republican activist, regarding a petition on behalf of Thomas Whelan, who was one of a number of IRA members detained for their alleged involvement in the killings on Bloody Sunday in 1920. The letter is dated 19 February 1921; Whelan was hanged in Mountjoy Prison on 14 March 1921.

Opposite:
A proclamation announcing the calling of the 'Parliament of Southern Ireland' established under the Government of Ireland Act 1920, issued by the viceroy, and dated 4 May 1921.

By His Excellency the Lord Lieutenant-General and General Governor of Ireland.

A PROCLAMATION

DECLARING THE CALLING OF A PARLIAMENT OF SOUTHERN IRELAND.

WHEREAS by the Government of Ireland Act, 1920, it is enacted that on and after a certain day, to be fixed in manner therein provided, there shall be established for Southern Ireland a Parliament to be called the Parliament of Southern Ireland, consisting of His Majesty, the Senate of Southern Ireland, and the House of Commons of Southern Ireland.

And whereas it is further provided therein that the Lord Lieutenant of Ireland shall in His Majesty's name summon, prorogue, and dissolve the Parliament of Southern Ireland.

And whereas His Majesty did by Order in Council fix the 3rd day of May, 1921, as the day on and after which the Parliament of Southern Ireland should be established:

And whereas His Majesty is desirous and resolved to meet His People of Southern Ireland, and to have their advice in Parliament:

Now I, the Right Honourable Edmund Bernard, Viscount FitzAlan of Derwent, Lieutenant-General and General Governor of Ireland, do hereby make known to all His Majesty's loving subjects His Royal Will and Pleasure to call a Parliament of Southern Ireland, and do further declare that I have given Order that the Chancellor of that part of the United Kingdom called Ireland do upon notice thereof forthwith issue Writs in His Majesty's name under the Great Seal of Ireland in due form and according to Law for calling a Parliament of Southern Ireland to meet at the City of Dublin, on Tuesday, the 28th day of June next.

And I do hereby also by this Proclamation require Writs forthwith to be issued under the Great Seal of Ireland accordingly by the said Chancellor for causing the Senators and Commons who are to serve in the said Parliament to be duly returned to and give their Attendance in His Majesty's said Parliament on Tuesday, the 28th day of June next, which Writs are to be returnable in due course of law.

Given at His Majesty's Castle of Dublin this 4th day of May, 1921.

FITZALAN OF DERWENT.

GOD SAVE THE KING.

15187. (44.) 3. 5000. 5. 1921.   Printed for His Majesty's Stationery Office by A. THOM & CO., Ltd., Dublin.

the Auxiliaries beat their swords into ploughshares, and Lancia lorries, instead of bearing them forth from the Castle gates clad in the panoply of war, sallied out on the more peaceful errands of bearing towel-girt warriors to the pellucid depths of the forty-foot at Sandycove.[62]

In September Todd Andrews was surprised to find the life of the city proceeding with total indifference to what were to him 'the great issues of peace or war'. Theatres and cinemas were busy; race meetings ('racing people were exceptionally low in my scale of values') were being held across the country; Andrews 'began to wonder did it really matter to the man in the street whether the British stayed or got out'.[63]

Opposite and below: Auxiliaries, British soldiers, civilians and a dog outside the gate to the Lower Castle Yard on the day of the Truce, 11 July 1921, possibly in anticipation of a public announcement. Members of the public are seen in the second image congregating on Dame Street in front of the Olympia theatre, looking towards the Castle gates. The atmosphere seems relaxed.

Yet this was the issue that lurked in the background. The day after the Treaty was signed in December the *Freeman's Journal* despatched a correspondent to the Castle, where they were told by an official that 'there is nothing new here.'

'Not yet?'

'Oh, not yet, of course.'

The paper reported 'an air of vacancy and spiritlessness' in the Castle. Just inside the gate,

Two Black and Tans were sparring and chaffing each other in Cockney accents. Beyond them was the blank emptiness of the lower yard, relieved only by an infantry officer who, with cane under arm and hands behind back, strolled rather dejectedly in the direction of Headquarters. The bustle of the Irish war days had departed.[64]

It was, the report continued, 'the interregnum…for the moment the Castle is awaiting orders'. The impression of an era being brought to an end was reinforced by other changes, as the security around the Castle was gradually dismantled. On 10 January 1922 Mark Sturgis noted in his diary that 'The Castle makes a good propaganda appearance with its gate standing open for the first time in at least two years and soldiers busy removing barbed wire.'[65] They did so with good reason. By the time he was writing this in his diary, there was an identifiable pro-Treaty camp. The newly open gates of the Castle were presaging both a British withdrawal from Ireland and a handover of power to the supporters of the Treaty.

Opposite: 'In the castle': cartoon produced for the *Freeman's Journal* (10 January 1922) by its cartoonist 'Shemus' (Ernest Forbes). It depicts General Neville Macready reading a copy of the *Freeman's Journal* while an armed Black and Tan peers over his shoulder. The caption ran: 'The Black and Tan: "Any orders to-day, sir?". General Macready: "Pack your kit and stand by to embark."'

Before Dublin Castle could be handed over, however, there had to exist an administration to hand it over to. The solution to this conundrum lay in the text of the Treaty signed on 6 December 1921, which specified that a 'Provisional Government' would be established in Ireland to oversee the transition of power, and that 'the British Government shall take the steps necessary to transfer to such Provisional Government the powers and machinery requisite for the discharge of its duties'. By the morning of 16 January 1922 such a body had been summoned into existence, and by the afternoon it was on its way to Dublin Castle.

Endnotes

[1] L. Paul-Dubois, *Contemporary Ireland* (Dublin, 1908), 187.

[2] This account draws on Christine Casey, *Dublin: the city within the Grand and Royal Canals and the Circular Road with the Phoenix Park* (New Haven, 2005), 348–61; Rolf Loeber, Hugh Campbell, Livia Hurley, John Montague, Ellen Rowley (eds) *Art and Architecture of Ireland* vol. iv: *Architecture 1600–2000* (New Haven and Dublin, 2015), 175–8.

[3] John (1167–1216), the youngest son of King Henry II of England, was created lord of Ireland in 1177, he succeeded his brother Richard I (the Lionheart) as king of England in 1199.

[4] John Gibney, *A short history of Ireland 1500–2000* (New Haven, 2017), 11–86.

[5] Thomas Burgh (1670–1730), Irish military engineer, architect and MP of the Irish parliament. Designed some well-known buildings in Dublin, including the old Customs House and Trinity College Library.

[6] R. Barry O'Brien, *Dublin Castle and the Irish people* (London, 1909), 33.

[7] G.A. Bremner, 'Stones of empire: monuments, memorials and manifest authority', in Bremner (ed.), *Architecture and urbanism in the British empire* (Oxford, 2016), 86–124: 87, 93.

[8] Aidan Clarke, *Prelude to restoration in Ireland: the end of the commonwealth, 1659–60* (Cambridge, 1999), 1, 108–11.

[9] Frederick O'Dwyer, 'Dublin Castle and its state apartments, 1660–1922', *The Court Historian* 2 (1) (1997), 2–8.

[10] Peter Gray and Olwen Purdue, 'The Irish lord lieutenancy, c.1541–1922', in Peter Gray and Olwen Purdue (eds), *The Irish lord lieutenancy, c.1541–1922* (Dublin, 2012), 1–14.

[11] George Moore (1852–1933), Irish writer who spent time in London and Paris before returning to Ireland in 1902 and becoming involved in the Irish literary revival. From a Catholic landed family; the family home, Moore Hall in Co. Mayo, was burnt down by anti-Treaty forces during the Irish civil war.

[12] George Moore, *A drama in muslin* (London, 1886), 177.

[13] James Murphy, '"Mock court": the lord lieutenancy of Ireland, 1767–1922', *The Court Historian* 9 (2) (2004), 129–45; Caitriona Clear, *Social change and everyday life in Ireland, 1850–1922* (Manchester, 2007), 84.

[14] K. Theodore Hoppen, '"A question none could answer?": What was the viceroyalty for, 1800–1921?', in Gray and Purdue, *Irish lord lieutenancy*, 132–57.

[15] O'Brien, *Dublin Castle and the Irish people*, 33.

[16] Fergus Campbell, 'Who ruled Ireland? The Irish administration, 1879–1914', *Historical Journal* 50 (3) (2007), 623–44.

[17] Augustine Birrell (1850–1933) British Liberal Party politician, chief secretary of Ireland (1907–16); he resigned in the wake of the Easter Rising.

[18] *Hansard*, HC, 7 May 1907, vol. 174, col. 83.

[19] George Chester Duggan (1887–1969), entered the British civil service in 1908, served in the chief secretary's office, Dublin Castle twice (1910–14, 1919–21). His article 'The last days of Dublin Castle', published in *Blackwoods Magazine* under the pseudonym 'Periscope' in August 1922, is one of the few accounts from inside Dublin Castle during this period.

[20] Sir John Taylor (1859–1945), assistant under-secretary, Dublin Castle (1918–20).

[21] 'Periscope' [G.C. Duggan], 'The last days of Dublin Castle', *Blackwoods Magazine* (August 1922), 137–90: 137–38, (hereafter cited as Duggan, 'Last days').

[22] Kevin O'Shiel (1891–1970), Irish politician, civil servant and writer. Assistant legal adviser to the government (1922–3), director of the North Eastern Boundary Bureau (1922–5), Irish land commissioner (1923–63).

[23] The Military Archives, Dublin, Bureau of Military History, Witness Statement (hereafter cited as BMH WS), 1770/2 (Kevin O'Shiel).

[24] Eamon 'Ned' Broy (1887–1972), member of the DMP, IRA and commissioner of An Garda Síochána (1933–8). While a detective sergeant with the G Division of the DMP, he acted as a double agent. He supported the Treaty and joined the National Army during the Irish civil war.

[25] BMH WS, 1280 (Eamon Broy).

[26] Alfred Milner, 1st Viscount Milner (1854–1925), British colonial administrator, secretary of state for the colonies (1919–21).

[27] *Westmeath Independent*, 24 January 1920.

[28] David Lloyd George (1863–1945), Welsh statesman and British Liberal politician, prime minister (1916–22); chairman of the British delegation that negotiated the Treaty.

[29] Ronan Fanning, *Fatal path: British government and Irish revolution, 1910–1922* (London, 2013), 206–9.

[30] Sir Warren Fisher (1879–1948), British civil servant, permanent secretary to the Treasury and first ever head of the home civil service (1919–39).

[31] Eunan O'Halpin, *The decline of the union: British government in Ireland, 1892–1920* (Syracuse, 1987), 217.

[32] O'Halpin, *Decline*, 209; see also Fanning, *Fatal path*, 222–30.

[33] Duggan, 'Last days', 147.

[34] Mark Sturgis, *The last days of Dublin Castle: the Mark Sturgis Diaries* (edited by Michael Hopkinson; Dublin, 1999), 18–19, 23, (hereafter cited as Sturgis, *Diaries*).

[35] Ernest 'Ernie' Bernard O'Malley (1897–1957), Irish revolutionary, commander of the anti-Treaty IRA during the civil war and later writer. His memoirs of both the War of Independence (*On another man's wound* (1936)) and the civil war (*The singing flame* (1976)) are regarded as the finest personal accounts of the revolutionary era.

[36] Ernie O'Malley, *On another man's wound* (London, 1961 edn), 78 and 191.

[37] Sir John Anderson (1882–1958), British civil servant and politician, served as undersecretary of Ireland with James MacMahon (1920–2). He was governor of Bengal, India (1932–7), but is most well-known for his time in the British Cabinet during the Second World War when he was home secretary, lord-president of the privy council and chancellor of the Exchequer. British air-raid shelters, 'Anderson shelters', were named after him.

[38] *Oxford dictionary of national biography* (*ODNB*), entry for John Anderson (1882–1958), by G.C. Penden (available at: https://doi.org/10.1093/ref:odnb/30409; accessed 4 August 2021).

[39] Sturgis, *Diaries*, 105.

[40] Duggan, 'Last days', 168.

[41] Lt.-Col. Sir Walter Edgeworth-Johnstone (1863–1936), Irish sportsman and police official who joined the RIC in 1886 after a successful amateur boxing career. He was chief commissioner of the DMP (1915–23).

[42] BMH WS, 1285 (Eamon Broy).

[43] Patrick Moylett (1878–1973), Irish nationalist, founding member of the Irish Volunteers in Co. Mayo and successful businessman. His business provided a front to import arms into Ireland. He was Arthur Griffith's personal envoy during the Treaty negotiations in London.

[44] BMH WS, 767 (Patrick Moylett).

[45] David Neligan (1899–1983), joined the DMP in 1917 and later the British intelligence service, he was one of several agents in the DMP who passed on significant information to Michael Collins during the War of Independence, this garnered him the name 'The spy in the Castle' (which was also the title of his memoir published in 1968). He became the Irish National Army director of intelligence in 1923.

[46] BMH WS, 380 (David Neligan).

[47] BMH WS, 380 (David Neligan).

[48] Michael Collins (1890–1922), Irish revolutionary, soldier and politician. IRA director of intelligence during the War of Independence. Member of the Irish delegation at the Treaty negotiations; chairman of the Provisional Government of the Irish Free State (January–August 1922); commander in chief of the National Army (1922); killed by anti-Treaty forces during the civil war in August 1922.

[49] BMH WS, 1280 (Eamon Broy), BMH WS, 441 (Lily Mernin).

[50] BMH WS, 281 (Bernard Golden).

[51] BMH WS, 822 (W.J. Stapleton); BMH WS, 626 (John Donnolly); Duggan, 'Last days', 168.

[52] Christopher Stephen 'Todd' Andrews (1901–1985), revolutionary, writer and later public servant with Bord na Móna and CIÉ. Fought in the War of Independence in Dublin; on the anti-Treaty side in the civil war. He wrote two memoirs: *Dublin made me* (1979) and *Man of no property* (1982).

[53] C.S. Andrews, *Dublin made me* (Dublin, 2001 edn, Lilliput Press), 176–81.

[54] O'Malley, *On another man's wound*, 215–37.

[55] Eoin MacNeill (1857–1945), Gaelic scholar and nationalist politician; minister for industries (1919–21), minister for education (1922–5).

[56] Brian Hughes (ed.), *Eoin MacNeill: memoir of a revolutionary scholar* (Dublin, 2016), 110.

[57] Duggan, 'Last days', 170.

[58] Sir Mark Beresford Russell Grant-Sturgis (1884–1949), British civil servant in Ireland, appointed private secretary to Sir John Anderson in early 1920. He became a chronicler of events in Ireland from the vantage point of the Castle through his five volumes of diaries kept between July 1920 and January 1922, from which a selection was published as *The last days of Dublin Castle: the Mark Sturgis Diaries* (1999), edited by Michael Hopkinson.

[59] Sturgis, *Diaries*, 106.

[60] BMH WS, 441 (Lily Mernin); BMH WS, 715 (Frank Saurin).

[61] BMH WS, 1099 (G.C. Duggan).

[62] Duggan, 'Last days', 183.

[63] Andrews, *Dublin made me*, 206–7.

[64] *Freeman's Journal*, 8 December 1921.

[65] Sturgis, *Diaries*, 227.

Chapter 2

The 'handing over':
16 January 1922

The great fact is that the 16th January, 1922, will be written in history as the day on which the old *régime* ceased to exist and the Irish Free State took possession of Dublin Castle.[1]

There was a necessary prelude to what became known as the handover of Dublin Castle. The signing of the Treaty had split the independence movement and was debated acrimoniously by the Dáil in December 1921 and early January 1922. Even during the Treaty debates, Michael Collins had noted that 'I suppose someone will have to go into Dublin Castle to see what is there'.[2] The Castle and the government it housed were name-checked frequently in the debates; by Liam de Róiste[3] as 'an abomination', and by Éamon de Valera, who described the proposed Provisional Government 'as only Dublin Castle functioning by permission for the moment'.[4] On 7 January the Dáil had narrowly accepted the Treaty, but the British government had steadfastly refused to recognise the revolutionary Dáil and its underground government officially and would only accept the approval of the Treaty by a body that it did recognise.

In 1920 the British government had established two Home Rule parliaments in Ireland, one governing the newly created enclave of Northern Ireland, and the other governing the remaining 26 counties of 'Southern Ireland'. Elections for both were held in 1921. The resultant 'parliament of Southern Ireland' had briefly met, but with only a handful of members present; the majority of those elected in 1921 represented Sinn Féin and formed instead the second Dáil. The basis for the British negotiating with Sinn Féin in the first place was that, as victors in an election, Sinn Féin members were thus considered the genuine representatives of nationalist Ireland. As far as British law was concerned, however, what they styled themselves after being elected was a moot point. On the other hand, the British recognised that insisting on a meeting of the 'parliament of Southern Ireland' was an obnoxious prospect for republicans, so instead, the wording of the Treaty stipulated that the agreement would be ratified by 'a meeting summoned for the purpose of the

Michael Collins looking tired but relaxed, with his hands in pockets, at the Gresham Hotel, Dublin, the night the Treaty was ratified, 7 January 1922.

members elected to sit in the House of Commons of Southern Ireland'.

Those supporters of the Treaty who had been elected to the 'parliament of Southern Ireland' would have to meet, but not as the parliament to which they had been elected; a subtle but important distinction. On Saturday, 14 January 1922, a week after the Dáil ratified the Treaty, 66 of the 128 members nominally elected to the House of Commons of Southern Ireland—mainly the cohort of TDs who had accepted the Treaty in the Dáil—assembled in the Oak Room of the Mansion House for an event that took less than an hour. The building was surrounded by press and a small number of anti-Treaty protestors. In a sign that perhaps hinted at an expectation of a commotion outside, the library of the Royal Irish Academy, next door to the Mansion House, recorded no visitors for the first time since the beginning of the year.

The *Freeman's Journal* reported that the proceedings were conducted, to some degree, in Irish as 'the Gaelic state made its first appearance in Irish official life', with the unfamiliar terms *Rialtas Sealadach* (Provisional Government) and *Saorstát Éireann* (Irish Free State) being used. Alongside the pro-Treaty representatives were the four independent unionists elected for Trinity College Dublin, two of whom, E.H. D'Alton and Gerald Fitzgibbon, answered the roll call in Irish in what was noted in the press as a conciliatory gesture.

Motions for the approval of the Treaty and the constitution of a Provisional Government were proposed and passed unanimously. The chairman of the Provisional Government was Michael Collins; the other members were W.T. Cosgrave,[5] Éamonn Duggan,[6] P.J. Hogan,[7] Fionán Lynch,[8] Joseph McGrath,[9] Eoin MacNeill and Kevin O'Higgins.[10] Arthur Griffith had been elected as president of the Dáil to replace de Valera after the vote on the Treaty but would not be a member of the new body; he stated that the Dáil would remain in existence until the terms of the Treaty had been implemented.[11]

The Treaty stipulated that the Provisional Government had to signify its acceptance of the agreement in writing; and on the afternoon of 14

January Winston Churchill[12] had sent a telegram to Lloyd George informing him that the members of the new Provisional Government were expected to go to the Castle imminently to sign the necessary declaration accepting the terms of the Treaty.[13] They were to do so in the presence of the king's representative. The incumbent viceroy was, by now, Edmund FitzAlan Howard (created Viscount FitzAlan of Derwent for the role),[14] the first Catholic viceroy since the seventeenth century and considered the highest-ranking English Catholic layman of the time. FitzAlan, a former Tory chief whip, had replaced the marginalised and redundant Viscount John French[15] in April 1921, and was assured, if not convinced, by Lloyd George that an appointment to Ireland would be 'a nice, quiet, tranquil task'.[16] The appointment of a Catholic viceroy reputedly prompted the Catholic primate, Cardinal Michael Logue, to suggest that Ireland might next expect a Catholic hangman, but it was viewed by London as a conciliatory gesture in the context of the inexorable moves towards a settlement and a British withdrawal from 'Southern Ireland'.

The British withdrawal would begin as soon as the Provisional Government was in place. The demobilisation of the Auxiliary Division had started on 13 January. Orders for the closure of brigade headquarters in Sligo, Tullamore, Castlebar, Tipperary and Bantry had already been issued.[17] Troop withdrawals were expected to begin in earnest early the following week, with stores and ships being readied for departure at Dublin's North Wall.[18] The signing of the Treaty had led to traffic going both ways. On the same day on which the Provisional Government was formed, republican prisoners released from jail in the UK sailed to Dublin, from where they returned to their homes across the country; a detachment of these returnees arrived in Dún Laoghaire at the same time as the British military were preparing to evacuate the township.[19]

Following pages: Pro-Treaty members elected to the 'parliament of Southern Ireland' pictured at the Mansion House, 14 January 1922, having met to formally accept the Treaty and appoint a Provisional Government, many of the members of which can be seen in the front row.

The official British assessment of the 'state of Ireland' in the week prior to the handover of Dublin Castle recorded a country in a relatively peaceful state. There were various minor disturbances reported, such as an assault on an RIC constable in Dungarvan, or the disarming of three army officers in Cork by members of the IRA who were enforcing a decree against shooting game, but who assured the officers they would get the weapons back. That said, there had been a notable increase in ordinary crime, especially 'highway robbery and housebreaking', which would have to be dealt with by the authorities, whoever they might be. These crimes may have been relatively minor issues in the grand scheme of things, but their existence pointed to problems on the horizon; a period of limbo was emerging in which the British were about to leave, but who, or what, was going to take their place?

The British administration was very conscious of republican opposition to the Treaty, recording various incidents in which weapons and equipment had been stolen from the army and the police; presumably, they could not be sure that such material was not being taken by anti-Treaty republicans. Arthur Griffith's election as president of the Dáil in place of Éamon de Valera had headed off any prospects of a rival 'de jure Republican government claiming authority', but the transfer of power had to take place speedily, along with a 'direct appeal to the electorate' to secure the legitimacy of the incoming regime. And, above all, the chief secretary for Ireland, Hamar Greenwood[20] argued to his colleagues in the British Cabinet,

> there should be no unavoidable delay in carrying through the evacuation of the Crown Forces from Ireland, and thus demonstrating in the most effectual manner to the Irish people that the Treaty is a reality, and marks the renunciation forever of the British Government's claim to interfere in the internal government of their country.[21]

The Treaty had been approved in Westminster on 16 December. One issue soon apparent was that the British government had no legal basis to appoint a Provisional Government in line with what the Treaty stipulated; it could legislate for such a body, but this would take some time, and so a solution had to be found in the meantime. A transitional period was essential, as a sudden transfer of power to 'leaders who have till lately been in open rebellion against the Government they served' could lead to very serious problems; Sir John Anderson was particularly concerned about how the rank-and-file of the RIC would respond to this. So another solution was proposed by Sir Francis Greer,[22] one that 'should be done as informally as possible':

> the Lord Lieutenant might issue a proclamation stating that he had appointed certain persons to be a Committee to aid and advise him in relation to the administration of Irish services in Southern Ireland, and might make arrangements under which the heads of the different Government Departments were to act under the direction of the committee. In substance this would act as a transfer of the powers of the Lord Lieutenant and the Chief Secretary to a provisional government.

As finessed by Lionel Curtis,[23] the proposal meant that 'the viceroy would send for the most influential Irish leader who is ready to accept the Treaty, and would ask him to form a committee of his colleagues' to advise the viceroy, which would give a legal veneer to the transfer of power to the Provisional Government until the British could legislate to officially establish it.[24] Understandably, this was not publicised.

By the second week of January no word had come from Dublin Castle to the pro-Treaty leadership about any likely arrangements; they were still waiting for instructions from London. It had been reported, however, on Friday, 13 January that there was a 'general plan' for the

Castle to be handed over after Saturday, and within forty-eight hours if need be. Documents and even furniture were already being readied for departure.[25] Speaking to a journalist from the *Chicago Tribune* on Saturday, 14 January, Collins himself seemed to acknowledge the need for a smooth transition, saying that

> there is no question of sacking the staff in existing departments. I suppose our next step will be to walk into Dublin Castle, take possession and make a present of it to the Irish people. It won't be done today, but perhaps Monday or early next week, and no arrangements have been made as to whether it will take the form of a public ceremony or not.[26]

There had been, it seems, an attempt to move swiftly on the Saturday to confirm the appointment of the Provisional Government. FitzAlan had been contacted and was requested to come to the Castle for 3 p.m., only to find when he got there that Collins was preoccupied with a threatened rail strike and could not attend; a suggestion that three members of the proposed government could meet him instead was 'quite properly refused'.[27] G.C. Duggan recalled that the new ministers 'could not spare the time', and so FitzAlan 'did not propose a second time to subject himself to such discourtesy'.[28]

The precise procedures for a transfer of power were still unclear as of Sunday night, when an unnamed civil servant told the *Irish Independent* that it had not yet been confirmed that any ceremony would take place on Monday, and 'although it would be a very historic and significant occasion, there would be very little ceremonial about it'. The expectation was that the representative of the British government—probably the lord lieutenant himself, along with some of the heads of government departments—would meet Collins and the other members of the Provisional Government, probably in the Privy Council Chamber, in what was expected to be a short but formal ceremony. In accordance with whatever formula was settled upon, 'control of the government of Ireland' would be handed over to the Provisional Government. From that point on, it would be in charge. The anonymous official accepted that civil servants could all be sacked but, as Collins had suggested, this was highly unlikely (at least in the short term) 'as the work of the departments will have to be carried on'.[29] In line with what Collins seems to have implied, continuity was to underpin the change. Those departments that were to be withdrawn were 'packed up and ready to go' and would evacuate as soon as they were requested to do so, though it seems that at least some of what they could not bring with them would not be left behind either. In Dublin Castle a 'huge bonfire of "wastepaper"' was lit on Saturday 'in the courtyard beyond the upper castle yard'. According to Eamon Broy, included in the pyre were the files of the DMP's G Division. There had been concerns that transferring sensitive documents relating to 'political crime' to the new regime could place individuals in danger. Large quantities of police files were, however, also transferred to London.[30]

On the morning of Monday, 16 January, the Dáil government met in the Mansion House, where it considered some outstanding business before adjourning. It would not meet again until 24 January and, in the meantime, the new Provisional Government took centre stage, as it held its first meeting in the same place at 11 a.m.[31] Present were Michael Collins, W.T. Cosgrave, Éamonn Duggan, Patrick Hogan, Fionán Lynch, Joe McGrath, Eoin MacNeill and Kevin O'Higgins (all names were recorded in Irish). Griffith played no official part in the new administration. There was a certain sleight of hand here: Griffith would play a lead role in negotiations with the British throughout 1922. By remaining at the head of the Dáil and maintaining the existence of its government, even if members of that government were never formally recognised by the British, he could ensure that their legitimacy could be defended by retaining a continuity with the Dáil that had approved the Treaty. The impression of a politically useful link between the Dáil and the new Provisional Government was given by the composition of

Rialtas Sealadach na hÉireann

16th. Jany 1922   Minutes of meeting held at Mansion House
11 am.   Dublin

Attendance.

There were present Micheal O Coileáin, Liam T. Mac
Coxgair, Eamon O Dúgáin, Padraig O hOgáin, Fionán O Loingsigh
Seosamh Mag Craith, Eoin Mac Neill and Caoimhghin O hUigín

1. Appointment of Chairman.

On the proposal of Eoin Mac Neill, Micheal
O Coileáin was elected Chairman of the Irish Provisional
Government.

2. Arrangements for taking over Functions.

Arrangements were made to visit Dublin Castle
at 1.40 pm. in the afternoon for the purpose of taking over the
various Departments of State.

Adjournment.

The meeting adjourned to 4 pm.

Chairman.

Minutes of the first
meeting of the Irish
Provisional Government
('Rialtas Sealadach na
hÉireann') in the Mansion
House on 16 January 1922.
The handwriting appears to
be that of Michael Collins.
The second point on the
agenda reads 'Arrangements
were made to visit Dublin
Castle at 1.40 p.m. in the
afternoon for the purpose
of taking over the various
Departments of State.'

this new body: there was considerable overlap between the Dáil ministry and that of the Provisional Government, with some members of one holding the same positions in the other. Indeed, the two bodies would eventually coalesce, but in the unique circumstances of early 1922 an ambiguous distinction served a purpose.[32] At the same time, the Provisional Government would begin the process of taking over power under the terms of the Treaty. Collins's new role as chairman of the Provisional Government would solidify his public role as a pro-Treaty leader.

The Provisional Government's authority had been exerted even before it was officially confirmed in any case when Collins intervened to prevent the aforementioned threatened national rail strike, arising from a dispute between employers and unions over pay and conditions awarded in an arbitration agreement. Greenwood later noted that 'their prompt and successful handling of this crisis has undoubtedly strengthened the position of the new Government in the eyes of the Irish public'.[33] When the time finally came, the agenda for the new Provisional Government's first meeting was straightforward: Collins was confirmed as chairman, and 'arrangements were made to visit Dublin Castle at 1.40 p.m. in the afternoon for the purpose of taking over the various departments of State'.[34] This was only settled upon at short notice by telephone on Monday, as Collins had been out of the city since Saturday visiting his fiancée Kitty Kiernan[35] in Longford (his return was apparently delayed).[36]

It was clearly impromptu; from a British perspective there were no plans to manage the event or consideration given to how it might be covered in the press. Yet it had been widely flagged in the press on the morning of 16 January—quite possibly at the instigation of the new regime—that Collins and his colleagues would in the next few days or even hours, be entering Dublin Castle as representatives of the Irish nation to deal with that hotbed of bureaucracy, tyranny, reaction and misrule in accordance with the wishes of the Irish people, now its acknowledged masters, and in their name to end forever the iniquities of 'Castle' so-called government.[37]

The Castle lay behind the intersection of Dame Street and George's Street, adjacent to the commercial district around Dame Street (in which insurance and banking quite literally loomed large) and the western fringe of the retail district centred around the more high-end shops of Grafton Street. Dawson Street was the eastern edge, and so the Provisional Government would have traversed both districts going to and from the Castle. Crowds had assembled near the Castle from early that morning, though they were unsure of what time the event was to take place. The DMP regulated the traffic in the vicinity. Barbed wire had been removed from the approaches to the Castle, and inside the complex some of the canvas screens erected for protecting the Castle buildings from view were being taken down.[38] The Lower Yard was filled with press, security forces and the families of officials, all reported to be waiting curiously, while on Dame Street and Parliament Street the crowd increased in size as time wore on, and 'with tense vision the people watched the movement of troops, officials, and vehicles coming and going...There was a general air of breaking up about the place'.[39] The size of the crowd around the gate to the Lower Yard at Palace Street made it difficult for military and official vehicles to get through.

Opposite: Members of F Company of the Auxiliary Division of the RIC being addressed by Major-General Gerald Boyd, commander of the Dublin military district, in the Lower Castle Yard, outside the Chapel Royal, prior to their demobilisation on the morning of 16 January 1922.

The Castle guard on parade in the Upper Castle Yard prior to assuming duties on the same afternoon.

The Palace Street
gate of the Castle,
armoured and
loopholed, with a
British sentry on
guard duty watching
prior to the arrival
of the Provisional
Government,
16 January 1922.
The fringe of a canvas
screen to block views
into the Castle is
visible at the top of
the picture.

Activity mounted throughout the morning and into the afternoon. At around 11.30 a.m. 'a stir was created' as the members of F Company of the Auxiliary Division paraded prior to their disbandment, about which they seemed to be pleased. W.E. Wylie,[40] the legal advisor to the Castle government, arrived at 12 midday, as arrangements were still being confirmed; he was reportedly engaged in 'official conversations'.[41] Batt O'Connor,[42] while mingling among the crowd within the Castle grounds, overheard two 'English officers in mufti' reminisce about their experience in Dublin during the Easter Rising; one of them grumbled that with conflict brewing over the Treaty, he thought it likely he would be back in Dublin within a few months.[43] At around 12.30 p.m. word went around that the final arrangements were still being confirmed, but that FitzAlan was expected at the Castle at 1.30 p.m. The posting of what was erroneously reported as the last guard at the Castle just before 1 p.m. proved to be of particular interest to onlookers on what was a crisp, cold day; perhaps twenty soldiers, with at least one machine gun, marched from Ship Street Barracks to the Upper Yard, parading in front of the viceregal (now state) apartments facing towards Cork Hill before dispersing to their posts through the Lower Yard.[44] Numerous onlookers, journalists, photographers and newsreel cameramen were scattered throughout the Upper Yard in anticipation of the proceedings.[45]

O'Connor heard cheering from the direction of Dame Street as the members of the Provisional Government made their way to the Castle from the Mansion House. They arrived at approximately 1.30 p.m. in three cars (apparently taxis) followed by a horsedrawn jarvey and came through the gate at Palace Street before turning right into the expanse of the Lower Yard of the Castle. The interior of the gate was flanked by police, military, photographers and various civilian onlookers (some of whom were gently pushed back by the DMP after they waved their hats in the air to greet the arrivals), and even a few excited children.[46] In the first car were MacNeill and Collins, who was smiling as he passed through a crowd that was eager to catch a glimpse of him; in the second were Éamonn Duggan and Cosgrave, with the remaining members of the Provisional Government in the third car.[47] Auxiliaries among the crowd (presumably those who had been demobilised that morning) were reported to be in good humour; one was jokingly told to remove a union jack from his tam o'shanter, while others grumbled at being recalled to quarters lest they miss the show.[48] The three cars ascended the incline of the Lower Yard before passing through the arch that lay beneath the Privy Council Chamber and into the Upper Yard, where they pulled up to the door of the chief secretary's office, in the north-east corner. Collins was the first to alight from the cars and entered the building swiftly, trying to evade the many photographers in the process.[49] They seem to have arrived on time, although Sean Clancy, who was present as a member of the IRA, later recalled that a British official who commented on Collins allegedly being seven minutes late received the rebuke 'Blast you, sure you people are here seven hundred years and what bloody difference does seven minutes make now?'[50]

Collins was followed by Cosgrave, Duggan, Hogan, Lynch, McGrath, MacNeill and O'Higgins. Others were also present: Collins's secretary Sinéad Mason,[51] Michael Hayes, Desmond FitzGerald,[52] and other staff (including some whom the *Irish Independent* later dubbed 'lady typists'). G.C. Duggan described the incoming government as

> a motley assemblage: some in tweed caps and unpolished boots; others with the beards of yester-eve still fresh on their chins; others with long lanky hair, collars and ties *au peintre*. Mr Collins himself was first in the door, and though the red carpet had in its time been laid down in the hall and up the stairway for many strange personages, yet surely this was the strangest scene of all it had yet beheld.[53]

On ascending the staircase they were greeted by James MacMahon, who assured them that 'You are welcome', to which Collins replied, without breaking stride, 'Like hell we are'.[54] Emmet Dalton,[55] as the chief liaison between the British forces and the IRA, had arrived earlier and made his own way to the offices, while some IRA members discreetly made their way from the Lower to the Upper Yard. 'It was, perhaps, the first time an officer of the Irish Army ever entered the Castle, except as a prisoner.'[56]

Many of the clerical staff had been released to watch the proceedings and some were even taking photographs themselves; there was apparently 'a good deal of gaiety and fraternisation' in the Upper Yard.[57] Some of the numerous journalists present were struck by the encounter between Desmond FitzGerald and his counterpart Basil Clarke;[58] FitzGerald

> was recalling his previous visit to the Castle under very different circumstances, when he was brought in at one o'clock one morning under escort, examined by officers in a room, and placed under guard in another place. The recollection had for him, however, no note of regret or complaint. It was, as it were, all in the day's work. [59]

No flag was flown over the Castle, even after FitzAlan arrived a few minutes after the Provisional Government, to more muted cheers.[60] He made his way to the Privy Council Chamber above the gate between the Lower and Upper Yard, the windows of which conveniently provided a very good view for the spectators within the Castle's yards.

> The simple stateliness of the Chamber with its two great brass chandeliers, pendant over the red cloth-covered table which occupies the centre of the room, must have impressed the new Ministers. The proceedings were private, but it is understood that the Viceroy, as representative of the King, received them as His Majesty would receive new Ministers. [61]

RIALTAS SEALADACH NA HEIREANN AT THE BRITISH

PHOTOGRAPHS BY TOPIC

PROTECTORS OF DUBLIN CASTLE PENDING THE ARRIVAL OF THE NEW PROVISIONAL GOVERNMENT'S FORCES : THE BRITISH GUARD INSPECTED IN THE UPPER COURTYARD ON THE DAY OF THE CEREMONY.

THE HEAD OF THE IRISH PROVISIONAL GOVERNMENT ENTERS DUBLIN CASTLE : MR. MICHAEL COLLINS ARRIVING AT THE PRIVY COUNCIL CHAMBER

TADEL IN IRELAND: THE "SURRENDER" OF DUBLIN CASTLE.

, AND L.N.A.

LORD LIEUTENANT OF IRELAND, WHO RECEIVED THE PROVISIONAL GOVERNMENT: LORD FITZALAN LEAVING AFTER THE CEREMONY.

A FORCE THAT MAY BE SENT ON POLICE DUTY TO PALESTINE: AUXILIARIES — THE "F" DIVISION ADDRESSED BY GENERAL BOYD (LEFT), IN COMMAND OF THE DUBLIN DISTRICT

FitzAlan met Collins privately first, before meeting the others, 'some of whom had six months before a price fixed on their heads or were spending a leisured existence in the walls of Mountjoy Prison'. [62]

The room and the seating arrangements were clearly visible from the yard. FitzAlan stood at the fireplace at the northern end, with MacNeill at the opposite end of the table and his colleagues sitting to the right of the viceroy's official chair. [63] FitzAlan made a short speech 'in

Previous pages: Photographic spread published as part of the *Illustrated London News* coverage of the events at Dublin Castle on 16 January 1922. Bottom-right: Crowds watch as Provisional Government members exit following the meeting in the Privy Council chamber.

Above: Edmund Bernard FitzAlan-Howard, 1st Viscount FitzAlan of Derwent (appointed on 27 April 1921), arrives at Dublin Castle on 16 January to meet the Provisional Government.

which he wished the new government success, congratulated them on their action regarding the threatened railway strike, and expressed the hope that they would lead Ireland into new more prosperous days'.[64] Collins was reportedly the centre of attention: 'Through the windows Mr Collins could be seen smiling and looking absolutely self-possessed as he met the viceroy.' The heads of the various government departments then arrived, entering from the chief secretary's corridor to the left of the chair. According to G.C. Duggan:

> The chiefs of the Irish Departments, all save Sir John Anderson, who, with great diplomacy, had found business in London too urgent, had been roped in, and now stood about the Council Chamber, for the most part obviously ill at ease, or regarding the proceedings with that air of cynical detachment which most responsible civil servants in Ireland are bound to cultivate if they intend to pass their life with some slight measure of enjoyment. It was a scene worthy of a painter, fit for the masterhand of some great dramatist. The drama of seven hundred odd years—was it comedy, farce, or tragedy?—was about to be played out; the curtain was about to fall on the last act and the last scene. When it would rise again it would not be on the same play. The characters, the situation, the stuff would be altered.[65]

The members of the Provisional Government were introduced to their counterparts in the Castle administration, with the encounter between W.T. Cosgrave and Sir Henry Robinson[66] deemed especially noteworthy ('the policy of one has been for the most part the direct opposite of the other's'): their rival departments of local government would surely have to be combined and would need to liaise in the interim.[67] Cosgrave had another unusual connection to the Irish administration, having been both prosecuted and defended by W.E. Wylie for his role in the Easter Rising.

Robinson's own account of the proceedings is worth quoting at length:

On the day fixed for the surrender of the Government to
Sinn Féin I received a telephone message to attend at the
Council to be introduced to the victors. I found on arriving
there all the heads of departments sitting on one side of the
Under-Secretary's room and the Sinn Féin leaders sitting
opposite, glowering at each other. I did not join the glad
throng, and went out into the corridor, where I was followed
by Mr Justice Wylie, who I suspect found it anything but
pleasant to be confronted with the new Ministers, most of
whom he had prosecuted when Solicitor-General for various
offences in connection with the rebellion. Inside the Privy
Council Chamber Lord FitzAlan was making the formal
abdication of the Irish Government to Michael Collins, and
having got through with this he left by the door to the State
apartments, and so avoided meeting his trusty and well-
beloved civil servants with a *sauve qui peut* ['every man for
himself'], which was the only advice he would have had
to offer them. After his departure the Irish Ministers des-
ignate were marched into the Council Chamber to join
Mr Collins, and took their seats around the council table.
James MacMahon then proceeded to call in all the heads of
departments to make them known to their new chiefs, and I,
being senior in the service, was called in first and was marched
round and introduced to each one in turn, just as a newly
sworn privy councillor is presented to the other members of
the Council. What struck me most was the extreme youth of
most of the new Ministers; they seemed scarcely out of their
teens, and all looked pale and anxious. No doubt they had
been through a period of terrible anxiety, and they certainly
looked gloomy and overpowered with the consciousness

of responsibility for the future government of the country. Michael Collins, their spokesman, however, was cordiality itself, and there was none of the 'top dog' attitude about him at all events. I was rather amused to hear people asking each other whether the civil servants would be expected to shake hands with men whose hands were stained with outrage and crime, but, if the civil servants had any doubt on the subject themselves, they were speedily dispelled by Michael Collins, who grasped their hands with his iron grip and shook them warmly with the greatest bonhomie.[68]

Robinson's use of language is revealing—'surrender' and 'abdication' speak for themselves, as does his suggestion that they were introduced as privy councillors traditionally were—but his recollection encapsulates an atmosphere of resignation, and weary distaste, with a smattering of relief. Collins was 'very active thereafter', as documents were exchanged, in what was later described as an 'informal occasion'.[69] As reported by Greenwood to the British Cabinet, the

> new Government…handed to his Excellency a copy of the Treaty, on which their acceptance of its provisions had been endorsed. His Excellency, after congratulating Mr Collins and his colleagues, informed them that they were now duly installed as the Provisional Government, and that the necessary steps would be taken without delay for the transfer to them of the powers and machinery requisite for the discharge of their duties.[70]

Its decisions were to be effectively rubber-stamped by the lord lieutenant, who would act on the advice of the new ministers; an adroitness intended to let them function legally until the British parliament could regularise their position.[71] The official British statement

Kevin O'Higgins, Michael Collins (marked with an 'x') and Éamonn Duggan leaving Dublin Castle after the British 'handover', 16 January 1922. The description attached to the back of this well-known photograph describes it as 'the "surrender" ceremony'.

issued subsequently wished the new Provisional Government 'every success' and expressed 'the earnest hope that under their auspices the ideal of a happy, free, and prosperous Ireland would be attained'.[72]

The meeting lasted less than an hour. At one point while the meeting was ongoing an armoured car 'coming from where Heaven and the erstwhile Castle Authorities alone knew' entered the Lower Yard, though 'even the "Ogsies" [a colloquial term for the auxiliaries] seemed to regard it as an intrusion on the harmonious function that was taking place in the council chamber'.[73] The senior heads of departments began to leave at 2.10 p.m. Robinson was the first, followed by the members of the new government who departed at around 2.30 p.m. amidst cheers and a welter of photography. Outside 'amongst the interested spectators were a number of ex-court martial prosecutors in mufti, a number of Castle officials, and several American visitors'.[74]

Cosgrave was the first member of the Provisional Government to emerge. They all wore hats and overcoats, some pulling on gloves against what *The Irish Times* described as 'a cold, raw winter day', others with cigarettes in their mouths. Collins seemed to try to avoid the photographers again by ducking between O'Higgins and the wall as he 'bounced out through the Chief Secretary's doorway and pushed Éamonn Duggan and Cosgrave into the leading car, evidently having had sufficient photographing during recent days'. MacNeill was the last member of the Provisional Government to leave, followed in turn by a number of others, including, quite possibly, the 'lady typists'.[75] Lord FitzAlan himself departed the Castle after 3 p.m., and was accorded a 'respectful reception; as he left via the lower yard', without any of the ceremonials that one might expect to have accompanied such an occasion.[76]

Following pages: The car carrying Collins and MacNeill passing through the archway connecting the Lower Yard with the Upper Yard as they leave Dublin Castle on the afternoon of 16 January 1922, following the meeting at which the Provisional Government accepted the transfer of power from Viscount FitzAlan. The meeting with the viceroy took place in the Privy Council chamber, directly above the archway.

It was all sufficiently informal for business to carry on as usual around it: a military lorry was outside the Privy Council suite, in the Upper Yard just west of the Bermingham tower, being loaded with 'an immense number of volumes, some of them, at any rate, of substantial antiquity'; the *Freeman's Journal* pondered: 'It would be interesting to know if they were amongst the records styled under the old regime "Confidential"'.[77] More prosaically,

Lord FitzAlan, Ireland's last viceroy, leaving the Castle after conferring authority on the Provisional Government, 16 January 1922.

the activity in the way of removing stores, bedding and documents went on with increased intensity, and the crowds lined up in Palace Street and Dame Street gave vent to their feelings with good-humoured banter, here and there interspersed with boos when Black and Tans and Auxiliaries appeared. The military were frequently cheered.[78]

The members of the Provisional Government made their way back to the Mansion House. They were accompanied by Batt O'Connor, whom Collins had apparently spotted at the Castle

> and invited that I should sit beside him and amidst thunders of cheers our four cars drove out through the multitude along Dame Street and right on to the Mansion House, where we soon after got busy on other national work.[79]

O'Connor recalled that upon returning to the Mansion House, Collins sought out Arthur Griffith and announced 'Griffith! The Castle has fallen!'[80] His excitement was real, and it was presumably around this time that Collins wrote a short but exuberant letter to Kitty Kiernan:

> I am as happy a man as there is in Ireland today. My thoughts just now are all with you, and you have every kind wish and feeling of mine. Have just taken over Dublin Castle and am writing this note while awaiting a meeting of my Provisional Government. What do you think of that?[81]

The Provisional Government officially reconvened at 4 p.m. and agreed a brief statement on what had just happened. Cheering crowds gathered outside the Mansion House, complete with a large group on a horse-drawn wagon waving a tricolour, and, having had no visitors for the first time in a fortnight the previous Saturday, the library of the Royal Irish Academy was again empty of even the handful of readers who might on any other day be relied upon to visit it.[82]

Minutes of Meeting 16th Jan. 1922 at 4 pm.

Attendance:

There were present Micheál O'Coileán, Liam T. Mac Cosgair, Éamonn O'Dúgáin, Pádraig Oh Ógáin, Fionán O'Loingsigh, Seosamh Mag Craith, Eoin Mac Neill, and Caoimhghin Oh Uiginn.

1. ## Report of Proceedings at Dublin Castle.

The following report of the proceedings at Dublin Castle was approved for issue to the Press:

S 1.

"The members of the Irish Provisional
"Government received surrender of Dublin
"Castle at 1.45 pm. to-day. It is now in
"the hands of the Irish Nation. For the next
"few days the functions of the existing
"departments of that Institution will be
"continued without in any way prejudicing
"future action. Members of the Provisional
"Government proceed to London immediately
"to meet the British Cabinet Committee to
"arrange for the various details of handing
"over. A statement will be issued by the
"Provisional Government tomorrow in
"regard to its immediate intentions and
"policy.
"   For the Provisional Government.
"   (signed) Michael Collins.
                    Chairman."

2. ## Appointment of Secretary and Asst. Secretary.

Diarmuid Oh Eigceartuigh was appointed Secretary to the Provisional Government and Kevin O'Shiel - B.L. was appointed Assistant Secretary thereto. 16 Jan 1922

3 Members to Visit London.

Messrs. Eamon O'Dugain and Caoimhghin
Ohuigín were selected to proceed to London on 17th
inst. to meet the British Cabinet Committee to
arrange for the various details of handing over.

4 Notice re Transfer of Services hitherto administered by
the British Government in Ireland.

Notice as approved to be inserted in Daily Press
on 17th January 1922 and to be printed on
Poster form for distribution.

5 Matters Deferred.

Consideration of the following Matters was deferred:

(a) Statement of Policy and Intentions of
Provisional Government.

(b) Setting up of Constitutional and Financial
Committees.

(c) Settling of Financial Policy.

(d) Memorandum from Liam T. MacCosgair
regarding the payment of Grants out of
Local Taxation Account.

(e) Premises.

Mr. Collins indicated that he would take charge of
the Finance arrangements and that Mr. Cosgrave
would be associated with him.

Next Meeting.

The Provisional Government meets again
at 12.30 p.m. on 17 January.

Previous pages: Provisional
Government minutes from
4 p.m. on the afternoon
of 16 January 1922, after
returning to the Mansion
House. They contain
the text of the statement
later issued to the press,
describing how 'members of
the Provisional Government
received the surrender of
Dublin Castle at 1.45 p.m.
to-day. It is now in the
hands of the Irish nation'.
What had modestly been
described as 'taking over
the various Departments
of State' at the morning
meeting had become
'surrender' by the afternoon.

Oppostite: A copy of the
notice issued later that
day by the Provisional
Government on the
'Transfer of Services
Hitherto Administered By
The British Government
in Ireland'. The headed
stationery and the address
suggests this was a copy
made later.

Later that evening there were scuffles near the lower gate of the Castle after a Union flag was seized from a lorry and someone tried to burn it; auxiliaries ran out of the Castle 'with what appeared to be pokers' and attacked the crowd. A young girl received a head injury, and the crowd was told to disperse by the DMP. Crowds gathered again from 8 p.m., after the incident with the flag, but had dispersed by 11 p.m. No soldiers were visible on duty at the Castle on the night of 16 January: members of the DMP and military police stood guard, with the latter purely concerned with soldiers returning to Ship Street Barracks.[83] Elsewhere in the city, there had been a steady stream of British military vehicles making their way to the North Wall throughout the day in preparation for their departure by ship. That evening B, R and O companies of the auxiliaries, from Dublin, Dunmanway and Mountjoy Prison respectively, along with other members of the regular British forces, marched from Beggars Bush to Westland Row accompanied by 'derisive cheering and booing'. The police band who led the procession, and who played 'Auld Lang Syne' and 'God save the King' before the train pulled out, got a friendlier reception as they left.[84]

The next day the Castle was quiet, with 'a general air of listlessness', and though some crowds gathered in expectation of something akin to the excitement of the previous day, they would be disappointed. As the *Evening Herald* noted, 'the ashes of the recent holocaust of the "secret

RIALTAS SEALADACH NA HÉIREANN

(IRISH PROVISIONAL GOVERNMENT)

Reference No.

....

HALLA NA CATHRACH,

BAILE ÁTHA CLIATH.

N O T I C E.

TRANSFER OF SERVICES HITHERTO ADMINISTERED BY THE

BRITISH GOVERNMENT IN IRELAND.

WHEREAS pursuant to the provisions of an instrument entitled "TREATY BETWEEN GREAT BRITAIN AND IRELAND – ARTICLES OF AGREEMENT" signed in London on the 6th day of December 1921 by the Members of an Irish Delegation and a British Delegation respectively, WE, the undersigned, MICHEAL O COILEAIN, LIAM T. MAC COSGAIR, EAMON O DUGAIN, PADRAIG O hOGAIN, FIONAN O LOINGSIGH, SEOSAMH MAG CRAITH, EOIN MAC NEILL, and CAOIMHGHIN O hUIGIN, and such persons (if any) as may be determined by the Ministers for the time being, have been duly constituted a Provisional Government AND WHEREAS the British Government has taken or is about to take forthwith the steps necessary to transfer to us the powers and machinery requisite for the discharge of our duties as such Provisional Government so far as the same have been hitherto held and exercised by the British Government NOW WE, the said MICHEAL O COILEAIN, LIAM T. MAC COSGAIR, EAMON O DUGAIN, PADRAIG O hOGAIN, FIONAN O LOINGSIGH, SEOSAMH MAG CRAITH, EOIN MAC NEILL, and CAOIMHGHIN O hUIGIN do hereby publish and proclaim that we have this day undertaken and entered upon the discharge and performance of the duties and functions of the Provisional Government constituted as aforesaid AND WE do hereby direct that all Law Courts, Corporations, Councils, Departments of State, Boards, Judges, Civil Servants, Officers of the Peace and all Public Servants and functionaries hitherto acting under the authority of the British Government shall continue to carry out their functions unless and until otherwise ordered by us pending the constitution of the Parliament and Government of Saorstat na hEireann and without prejudice to the full and free exercise by that Parliament and Government when constituted of all and every its powers and authorities in regard to them or any of them.
AND in the meantime WE do hereby prohibit the appointing, or the altering of the status, rights, perquisites or stipend, or the transfer or dismissal of any Officer, servant, employee, or functionary of the State without the specific authority in that behalf of this Provisional Government or the Minister thereof having authority from us in the particular case.
AND we do further prohibit the removal, tampering with or destruction of any records, documents, correspondence, accounts, books, writings, or papers of a public nature or relating to, or which came into existence for the purposes of, Government or Public administration in Ireland or for the purpose of any matter or thing connected with such Government or administration or any branch thereof.
PUBLISHED AT DUBLIN this 16th day of January 1922.
(Signed)
MICHEAL O COILEAIN.
LIAM T. MAC COSGAIR.
EAMON O DUGAIN.
PADRAIG O hOGAIN.
FIONAN O LOINGSIGH.
SEOSAMH MAC CRAITH.

EOIN MAC NEILL.
CAOIMHGHIN O hUIGIN.

and confidential" police reports were still floating about as though reluctant to leave their old haunts.'[85] The previous day's proceedings naturally loomed large in the press, who seized upon the drama of Dublin Castle's 'surrender', with Collins as the star of the show. According to the *Freeman's Journal*,

> the black old fortress of iniquity has fallen. And it went down in circumstances of abject humiliation, its custodians placing the keys in the hands of the one man in Ireland that the Terror had sworn to crush.

The correspondent mused, perhaps not unreasonably, that 'a little while ago and his head might have adorned a spike over the Castle gateway'.[86] The most important point that could be made was a pivotal one: 'the Castle as a garrison headquarters was gone; the Castle as a centre of the government of the Irish Free State remained.

"The Castle is dead: long live the Castle".'[87]

Opposite: Later that evening Dubliners could have celebrated with a night out! Broadside poster advertising performances by comedy acts Maidie Scott and the Nathano Brothers; performances by other variety acts, commencing 16 January 1922, included comedienne Susie Marney, singer Lillian Barnes and comedians Zoona & Milroy in the Theatre Royal Hippodrome and Winter Gardens, Dublin.

THEATRE ROYAL
HIPPODROME
AND
WINTER GARDENS.

Proprietors—The Dublin Theatre Co., Ltd.　　　**DUBLIN.**　　　Director of Entertainments—Mr. D. J. CLARKE
Resident Manager—Mr. J. H. HAMILTON.　　　　　　　　　Musical Director—Mr. W. SNELL ROBINSON.

MONDAY, JAN. 16th, 1922
TWO PERFORMANCES - 6-45 & 9-0

MAIDIE SCOTT
Just a Comedienne.

NATHANO BROS.
Presenting, Just a Laugh.

SUSIE MARNEY
Comedienne, in her Latest Successes.

BERNHART AND YOUNG
"Fellows of Infinite Jest."

BILLY SUNDAY
The Comedy Week-end.

ZONA & MILROY
Entertainers, featuring Childish Chatter.

LILLIAN BARNES
In Original Songs, by R. P. WESTON and BERT LEE.

THE ROYAL BIOSCOPE
Always Up-to-Date and Interesting.

THE
THREE ERNESTS
In their Comedy Gymnastic Novelty, "SPRING GARDEN."

GALLERY, 9d.; UPPER CIRCLE, 1/2; PARTERRE, 2/-; DRESS CIRCLE, 2/6; BOXES, 10/- to 40/-; SEAT in BOX, 5/-
Tax 3d.　　　　　Tax 4d.　　　　　Tax 6d.　　　　Tax 9d.　　　Tax Additional.　　　Tax 9d.

Children Half-Price to Dress Circle and Parterre, at 6-45 (1st House Performance).　Now Booking the Upper Circle—Box Office, Winter
Gardens, 10 a.m. to 6 p.m.　Later at the Upper Circle Entrance, from 6 p.m. to 8 p.m.
EVERY SEAT CAN NOW BE BOOKED IN ADVANCE.
The Management reserve the right to refuse admission to any person.　NO seats guaranteed unless previously booked.　No money returned.　Tickets sold
subject to the right of the Manager to make any alterations in Cast as may be rendered necessary by illness or any other unavoidable cause

WINTER GARDENS　VOCALIST DAILY BETWEEN 1 & 2 AND 4 & 5
TEA, COFFEE AND LIGHT REFRESHMENTS. OPEN 10 A.M. TO 6 P.M.　No Charge for Admission

Endnotes

1 *The Irish Times*, 17 January 1922.

2 *Dáil debates*, vol. T, no. 16, 'Formation of new executive', 9 January 1922.

3 Liam de Róiste (1882–1959), Irish politician, diarist and Gaelic scholar.

4 *Dáil debates*, vol. T, no. 16, 'Resignation of President de Valera', 9 January 1922.

5 W.T. Cosgrave (1880–1965), Irish revolutionary, supported the Treaty and was chairman of the Provisional Government following the death of Michael Collins (August–December 1922). Founding member of Cumann na nGaedheal and president of the executive council of the Irish Free State (1922–32).

6 Éamonn Duggan (1878–1936), Irish revolutionary and lawyer. One of the signatories of the Treaty, later Cumann na nGaedheal politician and parliamentary secretary to the provisional council (1922–6).

7 Patrick Hogan (1891–1936), Irish politician, minister for agriculture in both the Provisional Government and later Cumann na nGaedheal government (1922–32).

8 Fionán Lynch (1889–1966), Irish revolutionary, judge and politician. Member of the Treaty delegation, minister for education in the Provisional Government (April–August 1922), fought with the National Army during the civil war, Cumann na nGaedheal minister for fisheries (1922–32).

9 Joseph McGrath (1888–1966), Irish revolutionary and close associate of Michael Collins, travelled to London as his personal secretary for the duration of the Treaty negotiations. Director of intelligence during the civil war, minister for labour in the Provisional Government (January–September 1922), Cumann na nGaedheal minister for industry and commerce (1922–4).

10 Kevin O'Higgins (1892–1927), Irish revolutionary, barrister, Cumann na nGaedheal politician. Minister for home affairs (1922–4), vice–president and minister for justice (1924–7) and minister for external affairs (1927). He was influential in discussions on the evolution of dominion status at imperial conferences in the 1920s. He was assassinated by the anti-Treaty IRA on 10 July 1927.

11 National Archives, Ireland, Department of the Taoiseach (hereafter cited as NAI, TSCH), TSCH/3/S1, 'Meeting of parliamentary representatives held in Mansion House Dublin, 14.1.22'; *Irish Independent*, 16 January 1922; *The Irish Times*, 16 January 1922.

12 Winston Churchill (1874–1965), British Liberal and Conservative politician and two-term prime minister (1940–5 and 1951–5); a lifelong staunch imperialist, during this period Churchill served as colonial secretary and as part of the British delegation that negotiated the Treaty.

13 Churchill Papers, Churchill Archives Centre, Churchill College, Cambridge (hereafter cited as CHAR), Churchill to Lloyd George, 14 January 1922, CHAR 22/11.

14 Edmund Bernard FitzAlan-Howard, 1st Viscount FitzAlan of Derwent (1855–1947), British Conservative politician and the last lord lieutenant of Ireland (1921–2).

15 Viscount John French, 1st Earl of Ypres (1852–1925), senior British army officer born into an Anglo-Irish family in Kent, lord lieutenant of Ireland (1918–21). His sister, suffragist, republican and later communist activist Charlotte Despard (1844–1939), was bitterly critical of his tenure in Ireland.

16 Quoted in Keith Jeffery, 'Vizekönigerdämmerung: Lords French and FitzAlan at the Lodge, 1918–22', in Gray and Purdue (eds), *Irish lord lieutenancy*, 215–32.

[17] The National Archives of the United Kingdom (hereafter cited as TNA, UK), Cabinet files (hereafter cited as CAB), 24–132–41, 'Report by General Officer Commanding-in-Chief on the situation in Ireland for week ending 14th January, 1922'. Kinsella, 'Goodbye Dublin'.

[18] *Irish Independent*, 16 January 1922.

[19] *Evening Herald*, 16 January 1922; *Freemans Journal*, 16 January 1922.

[20] Sir Hamar Greenwood (1870–1948), Canadian-born British lawyer and politician, last chief secretary of Ireland (1920–22).

[21] TNA, UK, CAB 24–132–5, 'Weekly survey of the state of Ireland', 11 January 1922.

[22] Sir Francis Nugent Greer (1869–1925), British barrister and civil servant, parliamentary draftsman in the London Irish office (1908–23).

[23] Lionel George Curtis (1872–1955), British writer and civil servant whose work influenced the evolution of the British Commonwealth of Nations.

[24] TNA, UK, CAB 43–2, 'Memorandum on the Provisional Government as contemplated by Article 17 of the Treaty', 10 December 1921. See also TNA, UK, CAB 24–134–59, 'Summary of arrangements for the period of provisional government in Ireland', 17 March 1922.

[25] *Freeman's Journal*, 13 January 1922; *Irish Independent*, 13 January 1922.

[26] *Irish Independent*, 16 January 1922.

[27] John Butler, 'Lord Oranmore's journal', *Irish Historical Studies* 29 (116) (November 1995), 553–93: 586.

[28] Duggan, 'Last days', 188.

[29] *Irish Independent*, 16 January 1922.

[30] TNA, UK, CAB 43–2, 'Memorandum on the Provisional Government as contemplated by Article 17 of the Treaty', 10 December 1921; BMH WS, 1284 (Eamon Broy). *Irish Independent*, 16 January 1922; Gerard O'Brien, 'The missing personnel records of the R.I.C.', *Irish Historical Studies* 31 (124) (November 1999), 505–12.

[31] NAI, Dáil Éireann, DE/1/4, 16 January 1922.

[32] Maguire, *Civil service and the revolution in Ireland*, 124–7.

[33] TNA, UK, CAB 24–132–38, 'Weekly survey of the state of Ireland', 20 January 1922; *Dáil debates*, vol. 2, no. 11, 'Irish Railways—statement by Minister for Industry and Commerce', 3 January 1923.

[34] NAI, TSCH/1/1/1, 16 January 1922.

[35] Catherine 'Kitty' Brigid Kiernan (1893–1945), from a prominent business family in Granard, Co. Longford, widely known as Michael Collins's fiancée.

[36] *Cork Examiner*, 17 January 1922.

[37] *Irish Independent*, 16 January 1922. Unless otherwise indicated, the following account draws upon press reports also on this date from the *Cork Examiner, Evening Telegraph, Evening Herald, Freeman's Journal, Irish Independent, The Irish Times, Manchester Guardian, New York Times*.

[38] *Evening Telegraph*, 16 January 1922; *The Irish Times*, 17 January 1922.

[39] *Irish Independent*, 17 January 1922.

[40] William Evelyn Wylie (1881–1964), Dublin-born judge, Crown prosecutor at the military tribunals after the 1916 Easter Rising. Law adviser to the government of Ireland in Dublin Castle (1919–20) and became increasingly critical of government policy. In 1923 he was appointed chairman of the Irish civil service compensation commission by Michael Collins.

[41] *Irish Independent*, 17 January 1922.

[42] Bartholomew 'Batt' O'Connor (1870–1935), Irish revolutionary and later politician. A close associate of Michael Collins during the revolutionary period, he handled money and hid documents for him.

[43] Batt O'Connor, *With Michael Collins in the struggle for Irish independence* (London, 1929), 187.

[44] *Evening Echo*, 17 January 1922; *Evening Telegraph*, 16 January 1922; *Irish Independent*, 17 January 1922.

[45] *The 'surrender' of Dublin Castle*. 1922. UK. Topical Films; available online at: https://ifiplayer.ie/the-surrender-of-dublin-castle/ (accessed 4 June 2021).

[46] British Pathé, 'Irish Free State. Dublin Castle symbol and citadel of British rule for centuries "surrenders" to Sinn Féin Provisional Government', 1922. UK. Available at: https://www.youtube.com/watch?v=pgiDMzcxyPo&feature=youtu.be (accessed 4 June 2021); *Cork Examiner*, 17 January 1922.

[47] *Evening Echo*, 17 January 1922; *Irish Independent*, 17 January 1922.

[48] *Cork Examiner*, 17 January 1922.

[49] *The Irish Times*, 17 January 1922.

[50] *Seven Ages* (dir. Seán Ó Mórdha 2000), episode 1, 'The birth of the new Irish state'; interview with Col. Sean Clancy. Sean Clancy (1901–2006), born in Co. Clare, he served as an officer in the IRA's Dublin Brigade. A supporter of the Treaty, he joined the National Army and enjoyed a long career in the Irish Defence Forces, rising to the rank of lieutenant-colonel. At the time of his death he was the oldest veteran still in receipt of a military service pension for his role in the War of Independence.

[51] Sinéad 'Jenny' Derrig née Mason (1899–1991), Irish civil servant and Michael Collins's personal secretary.

[52] Desmond FitzGerald (1888–1947), Irish revolutionary, poet, publicist and later Fine Gael politician. From November 1919, along with Erskine Childers, he produced the official gazette of the government of the Irish Republic, the *Irish Bulletin*, which garnered significant publicity for the Irish revolution abroad.

[53] Duggan, 'Last days', 188–9.

[54] BMH WS, 939 (Ernest Blythe).

[55] Emmet Dalton (1898–1978), soldier with the Royal Dublin Fusiliers, revolutionary and later film producer. A close associate of Michael Collins; he became director of military operations in the National Army in early 1922.

[56] *Irish Independent*, 17 January 1922; *The Irish Times*, 17 January 1922.

[57] *Freeman's Journal*, 17 January 1922.

[58] Thomas Basil Clarke (1879–1947), journalist turned civil servant, considered Britain's first public relations professional. Seconded from the ministry of health to Dublin Castle in 1920 to lead the controversial British propaganda effort during the War of Independence.

[59] *The Irish Times*, 17 January 1922.

[60] *Irish Independent*, 17 January 1922.

[61] *Cork Examiner*, 17 January 1922.

[62] Duggan, 'Last days', 188–89.

[63] *Cork Examiner*, 17 January 1922.

[64] *The Irish Times*, 17 January 1922.

[65] Duggan, 'Last days', 188–89.

[66] Sir Henry Robinson (1857–1927), Irish civil servant, vice-president of the local government board of Ireland (1898–1922). He was advised by Michael Collins to leave Ireland in 1922 as his life was under threat. He published two volumes of memoirs in his retirement in England, *Memories: wise and otherwise* (1923) and *Further memories of Irish life* (1924).

[67] *Irish Independent*, 17 January 1922; *Cork Examiner*, 17 January 1922.

[68] Henry Robinson, *Memories: wise and otherwise* (London, 1923), 324–26.

[69] *Irish Independent*, 17 January 1922; TNA, UK, Colonial Office (hereafter cited as CO) 904/180.

[70] TNA, UK, CAB–24–132–38, 'Weekly survey of the state of Ireland', 20 January 1929, 4. Acceptance of the Treaty was to be signified in writing but any documents in question seem to have been unavailable by September 1922; the assistant under-secretary at the Castle, Alfred Cope, stated that no written notification had been sent to the British government, but that the Provisional Government had confirmed its acceptance of the Treaty verbally: NAI, TSCH/3/S1. There was also uncertainty about whether there was any documentation relating to the handing over of the Castle, given the informality of the event: see also TNA, UK, CO 904/180 (15 June 1922).

[71] TNA, UK, CAB 24–132–1, 'Provisional Government of Ireland committee', 11 January 1922. The agreed formulation, confirmed on 24 January, was that 'the Lord Lieutenant be instructed to act on the advice of the Irish Ministers in respect of questions relating to the dissolution of the Parliament of Southern Ireland, and of all other non-departmental questions, and in respect of each department from the date of its formal transfer to the control of an Irish Minister': TNA, UK, CAB 24–232–48, 'Heads of working arrangements for implementing the Treaty as settled', 24 January 1922.

[72] *Cork Examiner*, *Irish Independent*, 17 January 1922.

[73] *Freeman's Journal*, 17 January 1922.

[74] *Irish Independent*, 17 January 1922.

[75] British Pathé, 'Dublin Castle 1922', available at: https://www.britishpathe.com/video/dublin-castle (accessed 28 September 2021).

[76] *Evening Herald*, 16 January 1922.

[77] *Freeman's Journal*, 17 January 1922.

[78] *Evening Herald*, 16 January 1922.

[79] University College Dublin Archives (hereafter cited as UCDA), P68/4 (3), Batt O'Connor to Máire O'Connor, 28 January 1922.

[80] O'Connor, *With Michael Collins*, 188.

[81] Leon Ó Broin (ed.), *In great haste: the letters of Michael Collins and Kitty Kiernan* (Dublin, 1996 edn), 105.

[82] British Pathé, 'Dublin Castle 1922', available at: https://www.britishpathe.com/video/dublin-castle; Royal Irish Academy, Library Admission Register, 2–17 January 1922.

[83] *The Irish Times*, 17 January 1922.

[84] *Irish Independent*, 17 January 1922; *Freeman's Journal*, 17 January 1922.

[85] *Evening Herald*, 17 January 1922.

[86] *Freeman's Journal*, 17 January 1922.

[87] *Freeman's Journal*, 17 January 1922.

Chapter 3

Ceremonies and legacies:
handovers and the
British empire

WAS IT FOR THIS THEY DIED?

Another view of the 'handover' of Dublin Castle, from an anti-Treaty perspective. This cartoon, published in April 1922, depicts Collins bowing before the 'British Governor' while the ghosts of the executed leaders of the Easter Rising look on. The caption poses the rhetorical question: 'Was it for this they died?' The implication is of a surrender by Collins to the British; the opposite of how Collins and supporters of the Treaty depicted the event. The artist, Grace Gifford Plunkett, was the widow of Joseph Mary Plunkett, who was executed for his role in the Rising and who is among those depicted.

The Provisional Government reconvened in the Mansion House on the morning of 17 January, and a surprising decision emerged from its deliberations: Dublin Castle would not in fact become its new home. Instead, Dublin's City Hall would be ready by 21 January, following evacuation by the troops who had occupied it since December 1920, and 'the new buildings' on Merrion Street—the Royal College of Science—were also earmarked as premises for the new administration; Cosgrave would ensure that sufficient telephones were installed. The meeting also considered the allocation of government departments, appointments to a committee to draft the new constitution, financial arrangements, the formation of a police force and various matters arising from the Belfast Boycott.[1] This was a taste of the administrative work that would characterise the process of taking over as the British authorities disengaged from Irish affairs. It was obvious that, irrespective of the commentaries in that day's newspapers, the central focus was now shifting away from Dublin Castle to the new premises soon to be occupied by the Provisional Government, and towards London.

The meeting also confirmed that two members of the government—Éamonn Duggan and Kevin O'Higgins, with Patrick McGilligan[2] acting as secretary—would go to London to discuss the 'general question of handing over'.[3] On 18 January they duly attended a meeting in the Colonial Office at 6.30 p.m. with a British delegation led by then secretary of state for the colonies Winston Churchill. They were introduced to the committee that would oversee matters from the British side, and over the next few days the two delegations met to clarify how, in practical terms, the governance of Ireland would be transferred from British to Irish hands.[4] A roadmap for the administrative handover of power was agreed on 24 January. Kevin O'Shiel was appointed as the 'liaison officer with Dublin Castle Departments' on 25 January, and over the course of the next few months the immensely complex process of untangling the myriad arrangements by which the British had governed Ireland for centuries unfolded.[5]

Civil war broke out between the pro- and anti-Treaty sides in June, but on 6 December 1922 the Irish Free State, as envisaged in the Treaty, nevertheless formally came into existence. Henry Robinson's recollection of that day was tempered by the reality of the ongoing conflict:

> No concourse of people anywhere, no flags, no jubilations, the crowds which had surged rejoicing through the streets a year ago, when the Irish representatives provisionally took over the government of the country from Lord Fitz-Alan, were conspicuous by their absence now that the final act and deed was delivered which made permanent the severance of Ireland from England under the Treaty.[6]

But if the 'final act and deed' came on 6 December, what had happened on 16 January? The events at Dublin Castle that day had been loaded with significance by many commentators. From our vantage point a century later, we have an image of what such events should look like; an image exemplified in Neil Jordan's 1996 film *Michael Collins*, which depicted a ceremonial handover in the Castle yard attended by figures bedecked in uniforms that, on the day itself, either were not worn or did not exist, and saluting flags that were never flown. As historian Martin Maguire put it,

> The takeover of Dublin Castle was a revolutionary event, but it was not a spectacle. At that time there was no precedent for British withdrawal from her colonies so there was none of the elaborate ceremonial to which a later generation became accustomed.[7]

Indeed, the only precedent was the loss of the thirteen colonies in 1783 and the creation of the United States in the aftermath of the American Revolution.[8] The expansion and maintenance of the British empire in the nineteenth century was largely—from a British perspective—a success story. The twentieth century, however, would see spectacular reversals, especially in the wake of the Second World War.

Situating Ireland within Britain's imperial history is a complex but worthwhile endeavour. Since the Act of Union of 1801 Ireland had been part of the United Kingdom, but as discussed earlier, a separate executive was maintained at Dublin Castle with a chief secretary and a lord lieutenant, an arrangement that existed in none of the other constituent parts of the United Kingdom, though it became the model for British rule in India.[9] Under the union, Ireland had occupied an uneasy position between its nominal status and that of an imperial possession or colony. It was officially part of the United Kingdom, with representation in Westminster (usually on a franchise restricted by social status and gender), but the experience of conquest and colonisation in previous centuries had left an enduring legacy in terms of the structures by which Ireland was governed, the subservience of its economy to that of Britain, the manner in which it was policed and garrisoned by the military, the maintenance of a distinctive Protestant ruling elite, and ultimately the centralising of political control in Westminster. Ireland had evolved into something very different, in these regards, from England, Scotland and Wales, and the imprint of earlier colonisation had survived the union into which it was never fully integrated.[10] The various, and well-documented, ways in which Irish people of all classes and creeds actively participated in the British empire should not obscure Ireland's double-edged significance as both 'an important link in the imperial chain but also a critical fault-line at the Empire's core'.[11] Irish nationalists sympathised with opponents of British rule around the globe precisely because they saw a parallel with what they opposed at home.[12] This was also true in reverse for those nationalist groups elsewhere in the empire who drew a parallel with Ireland throughout much of the twentieth century.[13]

In the late-Victorian and the Edwardian era, self-government for Ireland was increasingly seen by the British ruling elite as an issue with imperial implications. The Irish struggle for independence took place in a world that was being remoulded, if not turned upside down. This

DUBLIN CASTLE'S SURRENDER.

Viceroy's Humiliating Role.

HANDS OVER TO MICHAEL COLLINS.

Executive to Carry On.

At Dublin Castle yesterday the Lord Lieutenant received the members of the new provisional government, headed by Michael Collins, and congratulated them on their installation. The celebrated Mr. Cope was amongst those present at the transaction.

Subsequently Collins issued a statement gloating over the surrender," and announcing that he will make known the provisional government's policy to-day.

Various heads of departments of state were introduced to the provisional government, which announced by proclamation later its intention of keeping them all in office, without prejudice, in the meantime, and without any reduction of salary.

MR. COPE SEES IT THROUGH

Strange Visitors to Privy Council Chamber

VICEROY KEPT WAITING.

Yesterday saw the beginning of the realisation of Michael Collins's repeated desire to " get the English out of Ireland," when he attended at Dublin Castle, accompanied by his fellow-members of the " provisional Government," and was received by his Excellency the Lord Lieutenant (Viscount FitzAlan), who informed these strange visitors that they were now duly installed, and that he (the Viceroy) would take steps for the transfer of powers.

Crowds began to gather at the Castle gates from an early hour, and by noon thousands had assembled, packing the little palace street which leads immediately into the Castle yard, and stretching in each direction along Dame Street. There they stood for a further hour and a half before any inkling could be gained as to the intended hour of the " provisional Government's" arrival. The members of this body, it appears, were in conclave at the Mansion House, with the exception of Michael Collins, who had been spending the weekend in the country, and had not arrived in the city until late in the forenoon. The Dublin Castle officials on their part were

PUBLIC SERVICES

Ordered to be Maintained Without Prejudice.

NO TAMPERING WITH BOOKS.

Late last night the " Provisional Government" in Dublin issued a proclamation dealing with the transfer of services " hitherto administered by the British Government in Ireland." The names of the eight members were given in Gaelic. The proclamation read—

Whereas, pursuant to the provisions of an instrument entitled " Treaty between Great Britain and Ireland—articles of agreement signed in London on the 6th day of December, 1921," by the members of an Irish delegation and a British delegation respectively, we, the undersigned and such other persons as may be determined by the Ministers for the time being, have been duly constituted a Provisional Government ;

And whereas, the British Government has taken, or is about to take, forthwith, the steps necessary to transfer to us the powers and machinery requisite for the discharge of our duties as such Provisional Government, so far as the same have been hitherto held and exercised by the British Government.

Now we do hereby publish and proclaim that we have this day undertaken and entered upon

PALESTINE NEXT ?

CADETS' NEW JO

Trouble Over Dispersal Auxiliaries.

SCENES AT HOLYHEAD

There have been remarkable developments in connection with the dispersal of the cadet auxiliary division of the R.I.C.

These men were being conveyed from to Holyhead in parties of 100, more or less on arrival at the Welsh port they proceeded a vessel in the harbour which was being used as a dispersal depot.

On Saturday two companies of cadets, arrived from Ireland, refused to leave the actual vessel, expressing dissatisfaction with financial aspect of the disbandment arrangements.

Prior to their departure from Dublin had been conferences at Beggar's Bush Barracks with officers from Dublin Castle, and some members of the companies remained in Dublin for further parleys with higher officials.

DUBLIN CASTLE PARLEYS.

These meetings took place on Sunday official statement from the Castle yesterday morning said :—

" Right Hon. Sir John Anderson, K.C. behalf of the Imperial Government, accompanied by Colonel Winter, C.B., C.M.G., on Sunday received a deputation from the auxiliary division R.I.C., to hear certain representations subject of terms offered by the Government members of the division on its disbandment main object of the deputation was to establish a pooling scheme outside the contract term order to provide for those members whose contracts with the Government have expired who are therefore serving for some months still to go. The deputation formed that, if such a scheme could be established on a voluntary basis, it would have Government's cordial support, and possibly assistance from Imperial funds, but that the Government could not possibly entertain any proposal which might compel a man with an expired contract to pool the amount due under that contract. The delegates undertook prepare a scheme on voluntary lines, and Durlacher, on their behalf, thanked Sir John Anderson for receiving them."

An official at the Castle said, in reply interrogations, that certain Auxiliaries who to leave the demobilisation vessel at Holyhead, on receiving representations from comrades in Dublin, proceeded to their duties. The terms on which the Auxiliaries were demobilised prior to any pooling scheme as was now suggested, were, that men whose contracts had expired received a free £30, less £4 10s income tax ; those whose unexpired receiving pay according tract but not in a lump sum, however, estimates for the year would not provide the but month by month as though they were in service.

POOLING SCHEME FORMULATED

The Central News says that a voluntary pooling scheme has now been definitely formed. The Auxiliaries' delegates have also made did not go unnoticed by Irish revolutionaries, and arguably one of the reasons why they were confident that they could grasp and remould Ireland's present and future was that the same process was happening, increasingly, in regions such as Eastern Europe, as so many of the European empires fragmented in defeat. The British were also aware of how Ireland was intertwined with the imperial crisis they faced after the First World War. The debates on the Irish settlement in Westminster in 1921 (during and after the Treaty negotiations themselves) saw both its British supporters and opponents frame the settlement very publicly as an issue for the empire.

Many acknowledged the failures of the union that had supposedly made Ireland an equal component within the United Kingdom, while other British parliamentarians implicitly confirmed that Ireland was not an equal partner within the union by deploying the rhetoric of British racial and cultural superiority.[14] The Conservative leader Andrew Bonar Law[15] had even confided to the deputy secretary to the Cabinet, Thomas Jones,[16] that he had come to the conclusion that 'the Irish were an inferior race'.[17] And General Neville Macready,[18] the British general officer commanding in Ireland, did not discriminate between opponents and supporters of the Treaty in February 1922 when he described them as simply 'opposing savages'.[19] Such pervasive views on Ireland tallied with the equally contemptuous views held towards the subject peoples of the empire; to see such a view directed within the United Kingdom itself makes it unsurprising that Ireland could be governed and regarded as a colonial possession.[20] Such a view also belied the supposed unity implicit in the concept of a United Kingdom of which Ireland was, institutionally, a part.

Opposite: Headlines in the *Belfast News-Letter* from 17 January 1922, noting the 'Viceroy's Humiliating Role' and the 'Strange visitors to Privy Council Chamber'. The column on the right wonders if evacuating troops will soon be deployed to Palestine.

Following pages: British troops removing barbed wire from an approach to Dublin Castle, 16 January 1922. The wall of City Hall is visible on the left.

An armoured car enters the Castle, via the Palace Street gate, 16 January 1922.

On the face of it, it is difficult to discuss the decolonisation of Ireland (even if only in political terms) if Ireland was not formally a colony. It was a component of the United Kingdom that was in 1921–2 being ushered towards the status of a dominion.[21] But if the histories of the dominions form part of the history of the British empire and its dissolution, then Ireland has a role to play within that.[22] This contention is reinforced by the fact that British administrators later in the twentieth century regarded the withdrawal from Ireland as one of a group of earlier diverse examples by which they might be guided as they withdrew from other 'dependent territories'—a category in which Ireland was classed.[23] The Irish struggle for independence was not just a reference point for other nationalist movements; it was also a reference point for the British themselves as they were successfully and repeatedly opposed by independence movements elsewhere in their empire.[24] A crucial later feature of British withdrawals from empire was the way in which Britain sought to retain its prestige and a degree of influence in and over its former colonial possessions in the fifty years between Indian independence in 1947 and the handover of Hong Kong to China in 1997; a ceremonial handover became a central part of how it did so. The achievement of independence for India and Pakistan may have been the model for the ceremonies that came later, but there had been others before 1947, and the event at Dublin Castle on 16 January 1922 can be counted among them.

On that same day, George Gavan Duffy[25] had, in his capacity as minister for foreign affairs, written to John Hagan, rector of the Irish College in Rome, to assure him that

> The Republican Government will continue its foreign representation until the Irish people decide (if it should so decide) to accept the proposed Irish Free State, and I do not anticipate that the Provisional Government will make any attempt to appoint Diplomatic Representatives abroad.[26]

But a decision on this matter would have to be made sooner or later, and some months later the following passage, hot off the press in a book entitled *The British Commonwealth of Nations*, written by the Oxford-educated Australian historian H. Duncan Hall, caught his eye:

> It is, indeed, of the utmost importance that any scheme for the future government of the Empire should make allowance for a great deal of divergence of type. It is not possible to fit into any rigid common mould a group of heterogeneous communities; some of which are fully developed, others are still visibly immature; some, although ultimately destined for complete statehood, are at present in the earlier stages of political development, and others again (like Newfoundland, Malta, and perhaps even Ireland), by reason of their special circumstances, may never be in a position to assume the full and self-reliant statehood of a great Dominion such as Canada.[27]

Duffy had thumbed through Hall's work thoroughly and in March 1922 advised Irish representatives abroad to familiarise themselves with it, and with this passage in particular.[28] For Hall had encapsulated how Ireland had been viewed by the British world a mere two years before the Irish Free State would be created by the Treaty, becoming a dominion like Canada.[29] Ireland was not the first country to secure independence from British rule, but it was the first to do so in the twentieth century, and its departure set an example that others would follow. British politicians and administrators would learn from the process.

Following pages: Two images that illustrate both symbolic change and administrative continuity as power was handed over by the British to the Provisional Government. The *Dublin Gazette* was issued on Tuesdays and Fridays and was the regular bulletin of the Irish administration, first published in the 1660s; this is the final issue, dated Friday, 27 January 1922. It was rebranded as *Iris Oifigiúil*, the first issue of which, dated Tuesday, 31 January 1922, is pictured here. The purpose remained the same, even if the name and headline font had changed.

The Dublin Gazette
Published by Authority.

The Gazette is registered at the General Post Office for transmission by Inland Post as a newspaper. The postage rate to places within the United Kingdom, for each copy, is one penny for the first 6 ozs., and an additional halfpenny for each subsequent 6 ozs. or part thereof. For places abroad the rate is a halfpenny for every 2 ounces, except in the case of Canada, to which the Canadian Magazine Postage rate applies.

FRIDAY, JANUARY 27, 1922.

CENTRAL CHANCERY OF THE ORDERS
OF KNIGHTHOOD.

St. James's Palace, S.W. 1,
24th January, 1922.

ORDER OF THE BRITISH EMPIRE.

The following amendment to the list of appointments to the Most Excellent Order of the British Empire (Civil Division), announced in the *Dublin Gazette* dated 2nd January, 1920, is notified:—

Member.

For Geraldine, Mrs. Oldfield, Kathiawar, Bombay,

Read Josephine Margaret Watson, Mrs. Oldfield, Kathiawar, Bombay.

Lord Great Chamberlain's Office,
Palace of Westminster,
S.W. 1,
January 24, 1922.

All Peeresses on announcing their intention of being present on the occasion of the opening of Parliament on Tuesday, February 7th, will have places reserved for them if announcement be made at this Office before four o'clock on Saturday, February 4th.

Peers' Eldest Sons desiring seats in the Peers' Eldest Sons' Box are requested to make a written or personal application at this Office.

No strangers can be admitted except by ticket from the Lord Great Chamberlain.

Tickets for the interior of the House of Lords will be admitted at the Peers' Entrance.

Tickets for the Royal Gallery at the Victoria Tower Entrance.

Lincolnshire,
Great Chamberlain.

Whitehall, January 20, 1922

The KING has been pleased to give and grant unto Admiral of the Fleet Earl Beatty, G.C.B., O.M., G.C.V.O., D.S.O., Field-Marshal Viscount Allenby, G.C.B., G.C.M.G., Field-Marshal Lord Plumer, G.C.B., G.C.M.G., G.C.V.O., and Field-Marshal Sir Henry Hughes Wilson, Bt., G.C.B., D.S.O., His Majesty's Royal licence and authority to wear the Grand Cordon of the Order of the Rising Sun with flowers of the Paulownia, a Decoration conferred by His Majesty the Emperor of Japan.

Whitehall, January 23, 1922.

At Malta, on the 1st November, 1921, His Royal Highness the Prince of Wales, on behalf of His Majesty, conferred the honour of Knight Bachelor upon Dr. Filippo Sceberras.

RIALTAS SEALADACH NA HÉIREANN

Iris Oifigiúil

(THE DUBLIN GAZETTE).

Published by Authority.

The Gazette is registered at the General Post Office for transmission by Inland Post as a newspaper. The postage rate to places within Ireland and Great Britain, for each copy, is one penny for the first 6 ozs., and an additional halfpenny for each subsequent 6 ozs. or part thereof. For places abroad the rate is a halfpenny for every 2 ounces, except in the case of Canada, to which the Canadian Magazine Postage rate applies.

TUESDAY, JANUARY 31, 1922.

Final Notice to Claimants and Incumbrancers.

COURT OF THE IRISH LAND COMMISSION.

LAND PURCHASE ACTS.

Record No. E.C. 9914.

Estate of CATHERINE SOPHIA MORTON (Spinster) and others.

Queen's County.

TAKE Notice that the Final Schedule of Incumbrances affecting the proceeds of the sale of the lands comprised in the First Schedule to the Originating Application herein, parts of which have been sold, and the residue of which it is contemplated selling under the above Acts in fee-simple, has been lodged in the Examiner's Office of this Court at the Four Courts, Dublin, and may be there inspected together with the said Originating Application; and that the 28th day of February, 1922, has been fixed as the last day on which claims or other objection to the said Schedule of Incumbrances may be lodged, the 3rd day of March, 1922, for proof of claims before the Examiner, and the 7th day of March, 1922, for distribution of the purchase money by the Judicial Commissioner.

Dated the 27th day of January, 1922.

ROBERT C. K. WILSON, Examiner.

Porter, Morris and Co., Solicitors for the said Catherine S. Morton and others, 60, Dawson-street, Dublin.

Final Notice to Claimants and Incumbrancers.

COURT OF THE IRISH LAND COMMISSION.

LAND PURCHASE ACTS.

Record No. C.D.B. 9867.

Estate of THOMAS O'MALLEY, continued in the name of Kate O'Malley (Widow), as personal representative of the said Thomas O'Malley, deceased.

County of Galway.

TAKE Notice that the Final Schedule of Incumbrances affecting the proceeds of the sale of the Lands comprised in the First Schedule to the Originating Application herein, which have been sold to the Congested Districts Board for Ireland under the above Acts in fee-simple, has been lodged in the Examiner's Office of this Court at the Four Courts, Dublin, and may be there inspected together with the said Originating Application; and that the 28th day of February, 1922, has been fixed as the last day on which claims or other objection to the said Schedule of Incumbrances may be lodged, the 3rd day of March, 1922, for proof of claims before the Examiner, and the 7th day of March, 1922, for distribution of the purchase money by the Judicial Commissioner.

Dated the 27th day of January, 1922.

EDWARD R. WADE, Examiner.

H. Concanon and Fahy, Solicitors for the said Kate O'Malley, 21, Lincoln-place, Dublin.

Ireland was also not the only imperial problem faced by the British in the immediate aftermath of the First World War. Another was the ostensible 'independence' of Egypt, proclaimed on 28 February 1922 (a mere two months after the signing of the Anglo-Irish Treaty) when Britain formally relinquished the protectorate it had maintained there since 1882. Unlike in the Americas and the Irish Free State, independence for Egypt was more nominal than real, and the relevant ceremonials were concerned with the establishment of an Egyptian monarchy rather than with the celebration of Egyptian freedom.[30] Lord Allenby[31] had been appointed special high commissioner of Egypt after the outbreak of unrest in 1919, during which an Egyptian delegation or 'Wafd', which later became the Egyptian nationalist Wafd Party, had travelled to the post-war peace conference in Paris to seek recognition for their country's independence; Dáil Éireann had done something similar. The leaders of the Egyptian delegation, including the future Egyptian prime minister Sa'd Zaghlul,[32] were later arrested and deported to Malta, prompting widespread outrage in Egypt.

The ensuing Egyptian revolution unsurprisingly received a lot of attention in Ireland, and there was direct collaboration between Irish and Egyptian nationalists at the time.[33] When it became clear to Britain that, like in Ireland, concessions had to be made to Egypt in order to secure strategic interests in the area (namely access to the Suez Canal), it was decided to declare the termination of the British protectorate and appoint a loyal 'king' (in so doing overwriting the traditional term 'sultan'). There was muted coverage of these events in the British press, however, with the *Daily Mirror* being one of the few newspapers to detail what could just about be described as a ceremony, when Allenby handed over a new charter to King Ahmad Fuad I of Egypt. As he and Lady Allenby alighted from the train in Cairo,

In early 1922, as an interim measure before the Provisional Government's first newly designed stamps were ready, a series of contemporary stamps of King George V was overprinted. The stamp shown here was issued between July and November 1922. The overprint means 'Irish Provisional Government'.

three lusty cheers were raised. He inspected a guard of honour of British troops and then walked down the platform and greeted as many of the eager crowd as possible. Afterwards he inspected an Egyptian guard of honour outside the station, and then motored to the residency, escorted by aeroplanes. The road was well lined by Egyptians. Good order prevailed throughout.[34]

These genial scenes did not last, however. There were widespread protests by the nationalists against the continuing de facto British presence. Zaghlul eventually returned from exile and was elected prime minister in 1924.

In the same region, the British Mandate of Palestine—one of the spoils of the First World War obtained following the defeat of the Ottoman empire, and also the eventual destination for many of the British paramilitaries being demobilised in Dublin in January 1922—would cause further headaches for Britain. The decades following the First World War saw continuing patterns of repression and reprisals in Palestine (not unlike those in that occurred Ireland during the War of Independence). More significant, however, was the mismanagement of Jewish migration to Palestine in the 1930s and a total disintegration of law and order, including the 1944 assassination of Lord Moyne (of the Anglo-Irish Guinness family),[35] the British minister for state in the Middle East, by the Jewish militant group Lehi. Here is further evidence of Ireland's 'imperial duality' as both agent of and agitator against empire: many within the ranks of Lehi had been influenced by IRA methods. Palestine was eventually handed over to the United Nations (UN), and war followed the ignominious British departure. The evacuating forces destroyed police-dogs but tried to salvage equipment, 'from their locomotives to the last of the paper-clips'.[36]

What Ireland, Egypt and Palestine all have in common was that in each case British power was relinquished under a cloud, with no proper

he NEW PALESTINE GENDARMERIE : *And Other Near-Eastern Matters.*

The Palestine Gendarmerie (British Section) Paraded at Plymouth Before Embarking on the S.S. "City of Oxford"

management from the centre and certainly no orchestrated ceremonies to mark the transitions. The embarrassing loss of prestige entailed in all three cases was not the impression that the British government wanted to portray to the world; in later withdrawals from regions of its empire it would seek to avoid repeating these mistakes by managing the symbolism of British departure more assiduously.

In 1921–2 the maintenance of the empire was paramount for Britain. As Winston Churchill told an Irish delegation led by Arthur Griffith in May 1922, 'You will find that we are just as tenacious on essential points—the Crown, the British Commonwealth, no Republic—as de Valera and Rory O'Connor,[37] and we intend to fight for our points.'[38] Ireland was leaving the United Kingdom, but it was being admitted to a select club: that of the self-governing settler colonies of the empire— the so-called white dominions. In 1867 England had united three of

In April 1922, approximately 650 former Black and Tans and auxiliaries arrived in Haifa, Palestine and commenced their duties as the British Palestine Gendarmerie. Their suitability for an imperial policing role does raise questions about the nature of their deployment in Ireland.

HEADS UP!

No. 4.   29th JANUARY, 1922.   PRICE 1d.

For centuries England has been EMPIRE-BUILDING.

Her surplus population has provided Black and Tans for every dirty service.

Black and Tanism is the oldest profession in England.

It has built an Empire for her.

Imperialism is the Black and Tan ideal.

With Unity and Wealth behind her, England has overcome scores of Small Nations—one by one.

She boasts that she is never without " Some little war."

But she never takes on too many wars at a time.

She doesn't like big wars at all unless she can get the French or Italians to fight them for her.

IRELAND AND INDIA AND EGYPT WERE BEGINNING TO BE THREE BIG WARS.

By making a Provisional Peace with Ireland she could set 100,000 men free to crush the others.

Possibly she might get the Irish to take an interest in Empire-building—to take a pride in the Commonwealth of Anglo-Saxon peoples—for the present.

THE SAME GAME SUCCEEDED BEFORE WHEN THE TREATY OF 1782 BECAME A SCRAP OF PAPER WITHIN TWENTY YEARS.

She fooled us then in almost the same way as she seeks to fool us now.

ENGLAND EXPECTS MUCH OF THE IRISH FREE STATERS, and in return:—

" They shall be respectable for ever,

They shall go to the Castle for ever,

The Police shall salute them for ever."

SUBSCRIPTIONS AND ORDERS MAY BE ADDRESSED TO " THE MANAGER, HEADS UP, POSTE RESTANTE, G.P.O., DUBLIN."

its colonies, Canada, Nova Scotia and New Brunswick, into the dominion of Canada. The Constitution Act was passed on 1 July 1867; this date became Dominion Day, later Canada Day. In the southern hemisphere, the Commonwealth of Australia Constitution Act (1900) brought about the merger of the six original self-governing colonies and led to the adoption of an Australian constitution and Federation Day (1 January 1901). In both cases, and in contrast to the creation of the Irish Free State, a date was designated to mark the respective political transitions. The striking difference between those other dominions

An anti-Treaty pamphlet in circulation in January 1922, that clearly links nationalist movements in Ireland, India and Egypt together as having a destabilising effect on the British empire. The pamphlet ominously ends with a warning to the new regime that hints at the rhetorical power of the symbolism that accrued to Dublin Castle: 'England expects much of the Irish Free Staters…they shall go to the Castle forever.'

and Ireland by the time of the handover of power in Dublin in 1922, however, was that dominion status was reluctantly given to the Irish Free State as a *last resort*. Ireland achieved dominion status 'not by evolution but by revolution'.[39]

Gradual legislative change for the 'white' dominions had been forthcoming and they would gain full independence in their foreign policies with the Balfour Declaration of 1926 and later the Statute of Westminster of 1931. In the decade after the civil war, Ireland's pro-Treaty Cumann na nGaedheal government played a significant part in modernising the emergent commonwealth, moving it away from its role as an imperial body towards a grouping of likeminded, independent, sovereign states; this, in fact, became the hallmark of Cumann na nGaedheal foreign policy.[40] The old dominions were uncertain about these developments. Australia did not adopt the Statute of Westminster until 1942, so hesitant was it about full independence, mainly because of its vulnerability to attack by Japan in the Second World War. Geography played a significant part in how willing more distant dominions were to retain the link with Britain, while Ireland's proximity arguably had the opposite effect.

Many contemporaries framed the Irish struggle for independence in terms of the global upheaval that followed the First World War. Comparisons and connections were established between India, Ireland and Egypt around this time.

The Egyptian revolution coincided with the outbreak of the Irish War of Independence. Left: Egyptian women nationalists, demonstrating on the streets of Cairo, March 1919.

The 1919 Amritsar Massacre in India had an impact on Ireland and received considerable press coverage. Opposite: a cartoon, 'Progress to Liberty - Amritsar style' by David Low, linking events in Ireland and India in 1919.

Independence of a limited variety was *granted* by Britain to the dominions because it was strategically and economically in her interests to do so. By the early 1930s there was also recognition (only in so far as the 'white' dominions were concerned, however) that the unity of the empire could not be conserved by force for any length of time or in any desirable or profitable way, and that the task of realistic statesmanship was to conserve it by consent. Reginald Coupland,[41] the Beit Professor of Colonial History at Oxford, went so far as to suggest that there was value

Progress to Liberty-Amritsar style.

Reprinted from The Daily News,—Dec. 16th, 1919

in the magnanimity implicit in Britain's acquiescing to Ireland's 'radical' demands to dissociate itself from the commonwealth throughout the 1930s, which it did with the External Relations Act of 1936 and the 1937 constitution, and this culminated with Ireland ultimately leaving the commonwealth in 1949. Adopting such an attitude of concession, Coupland argued, would strengthen Britain's position in India 'and make it more likely that the Indian leaders will ultimately acquiesce in India remaining within the Empire'. Coupland anticipated the manner in which, in the future, by acting first Britain might pre-empt demands made by other colonial nationalists.[42]

The 1938 Anglo-Irish Agreements, under which Britain handed back the Irish naval bases retained under the terms of the Treaty (the so-called Treaty ports), can be viewed in this context. This occurred at a crucial time, as the relinquishing of the ports allowed for the adoption of Irish neutrality as a policy during the Second World War. Churchill, who had been conscious of the need to uphold British naval power during the Treaty negotiations of 1921, was said to have been furious with the then secretary of state for the dominions Malcolm MacDonald[43] for allowing such a thing to happen. The young MacDonald, then in his mid-thirties, played a part in a gradual shift in attitude in British politics in favour of self-government in the colonies. When he became colonial secretary during the Second World War, he brought to the task an open-minded approach and began to ask questions about Britain's 'moral prestige' in relation to its colonial policy.

This became especially pertinent in the aftermath of the Second World War, when Britain found itself unable to defend its global imperial system unaided. It was essential to convince allies that victory in the war would bring positive benefits to Britain's colonial subjects, especially given their significant contribution to Britain's war effort and the dominions' growing independence and influence on policy making in London. There were now huge obligations in terms of Britain's peacetime defence spending in order to meet the new threat of Soviet aggression in Europe and colonial emergencies further afield. As John Maynard Keynes[44] (then at the Treasury) put it in August 1945, 'we cannot police half the world at our own expense when we have already gone into pawn to the other half.'[45] The end of the war brought a major shift for Britain's empire, and led to a monumental event on a global scale, for Britain could no longer hold on to India. On top of decades of political unrest there, Britain was now also indebted to its colony, owing it in excess of £1,300-million. A British withdrawal from India was inevitable.

As we have seen, Britain had been faced with an imperial crisis across Ireland, Egypt and India in the wake of the First World War. After the Second World War it faced another, but it now had to deal with it from an unfamiliar position of relative weakness. In this new climate, with the world's eyes firmly in Britain's direction, a ceremony for handing over power to the subcontinent might serve as a very concrete and visible statement that power had actually been handed over. Considerable thought was given to the ceremonies appropriate to the transfer of power in India and Pakistan. The independence struggle in India was the one most commonly linked with that of Ireland, and in the post-war era, Indian independence would be depicted as a British rather than an Indian achievement, something arising almost organically out of her long-term policy; it would be presented in a way that vindicated British rule. The imagery of the grateful imperial subject and the wise and benevolent colonial master was a recurrent underlying motif in many contemporary press accounts.[46] The vast international press coverage of the opulent ceremonies was as much for the British public and the world audience as for those on the sub-continent. The personal management of this by the last viceroy of India, Louis Mountbatten[47]— 'Operation seduction' as his daughter Pamela later described it—was of pivotal importance.[48]

The first ceremonies were held in Karachi on 13 August 1947, where a state banquet was held, followed by a reception attended by some 1,500 of the leading citizens of Pakistan (who, according to Mountbatten, included some very strange looking 'jungly' men). The reception the Mountbattens received from the people of Pakistan surprised them, and on leaving Mountbatten reflected 'Miss Jinnah literally had tears in her eyes when she bade us farewell…even the austere Jinnah[49] himself showed some emotion on bidding us farewell.'[50] They returned to Delhi where the Indian constituent assembly took power at midnight on the night of 14 August. Mountbatten described the following day, 15 August 1947, as 'the most remarkable and inspiring day of my life. We started at 8:30 with the Swearing-In ceremony in the Durbar Hall in front of an official audience of some 500'.[51] They then drove in procession from Government House (formerly Viceroy's House) to the Council Chamber. According to Mountbatten, 'never have such crowds been seen' within the memory of anyone he had spoken to, the ceremony in the Council Chamber was 'extremely dignified', and his speech was well received. He thought the great event of the day was the salutation of 'the new Dominion flag' (the Indian flag), which took place at 6 p.m. This programme of events had originally included a ceremonial lowering of the union flag, but when Mountbatten had discussed this with Jawaharlal Nehru,[52] who was to become the first prime minister of an independent India, Nehru apparently

> entirely agreed that this was a day they wanted everybody to be happy, and if the lowering of the Union Jack in any way offended British susceptibilities, he would certainly see that it would not take place, the more so as the Union Jack would still be flown on a dozen days a year in the Dominion.[53]

The ceremony was overwhelmed by crowds, however, and after a hurried consultation it was decided that the only thing to do to alleviate the force of the crowds was to hoist the flag and fire the salute

as quickly as possible and abandon the rest of the programme. According to Mountbatten, in his report to London written with his flair for the dramatic, 'this was done amongst scenes of the most fantastic rejoicing, and as the flag broke a brilliant rainbow appeared in the sky which was taken by the crowd as a good omen'.[54]

Just like there had been in Ireland in 1922, there were plans for troop evacuations, and so the following day the Mountbattens went to Bombay to say goodbye to the first contingent of British troops to leave India.

This 1947 image shows Lord Mountbatten, Edwina Mountbatten and Jawaharlal Nehru at the first Independence Day celebrations in New Delhi. A report stated that Mountbatten and Nehru rescued children lost in the crowds by making them board the state coach.

It went off extremely well amidst scenes of great enthusi-
asm…the local police estimated the crowd as the biggest in
the history of the city. Several hundreds of thousands lined
the many miles of route…the demonstration was all the
more remarkable since the drives from Government House
to the Docks and later to the Prime Minister's party, were
not intended as events in themselves. The crowd definitely
shouted out, 'England Zindabad' (Long live England) and
'Jai England' (Victory England).[55]

If the event in Dublin Castle in 1922 was not depicted as a symbolic
milestone by the British, however, the evacuation of their troops from
Ireland in the early months of 1922 was seen by their political and military leadership as a concrete manifestation of the British withdrawal
in general. While the departures from barracks were often large events,
complete with regimental ceremonials, they were of a different nature to
the ceremonies one might later have expected to accompany the handing
over of political control and authority.[56]

By the late 1940s ceremonies along the lines of those that took
place in India were beginning to accompany the withdrawal from other
regions of the empire, and the British government was using an official
term for the process that these ceremonies exemplified: the 'transfer of
power'. This term appears anodyne at first, but it was infused with the
power dynamic of paternalism; the imperial centre had *decided* to transfer power to the periphery. As we have seen, things were not so clear
in Dublin in 1922, with the use by pro-Treaty leaders and the press of
terms such as 'handover', 'surrender' or 'takeover' implying that power
had been taken, as much as given (a point not lost on some British officials). The handover and withdrawal in Ireland may have been the first of
its kind for Britain in the twentieth century, but it was India that became
the template in the decades thereafter when Britain's empire began to
reduce apace after the Second World War. The 'transfer' ceremonies were

the last act in what became an official routine in getting a country ready for independence, regarded from a British perspective as a coming-of-age ceremony of sorts.

Britain would learn to anticipate local developments instead of reacting to them as it had in Ireland and Egypt in the 1920s. By doing so, colonial rule would be prolonged, to the benefit, as the Colonial Office saw it, of both Britain and the colonies. Arguably, the timetabled approach to independence that was adopted for Gold Coast (Ghana) in 1957 was the first step in creating a future 'informal' empire. The aim was twofold: to demonstrate that colonial rule could be progressive, but also to prepare for an orderly transfer of power to stable pro-British governments. In the end, timetables had to be drastically altered as the 'wind of change' blew through the African continent, but, as had happened in India, the symbolism of ceremony was harnessed where possible. The impression given had to be that power was being transferred voluntarily, with dignity and with mutual expressions of esteem and good will; that a member of the British royal family would attend, to set a regal seal of approval on the proceedings; and that Britain and its former colony would remain on good terms thereafter, with the former still wielding some benevolent influence over the latter. It had to be planned.

In the decades that followed, the British procedure for a handover of power across its diminishing empire would be refined and repeated. According to Sir Colin Allan,[57]

> there was a check-list of about eighty points under two main headings. They are ticked off in a bureaucratic way one by one—relevant or not—it is as simple as that. Only one or two will be so controversial as to require substantial negotiation. It has all been done, over forty times before!

There even emerged an imperial midwife in the guise of Colonel Eric Hefford, a retired British army officer who embarked on a career as a

Opposite: Ghanaian prime minister Kwame Nkrumah with President Éamon de Valera in Dublin, June 1960. (Note photo of executed 1916 leader Patrick Pearse; during his visit Nkrumah sought out a copy of Pearse's writings.) The first sub-Saharan colony to gain independence from the British empire was the Gold Coast (renamed Ghana). It was achieved in March 1957, after a drawn-out timetable set by the Colonial Office, which, after the Indian experience, wished to remain in control of the pace of change in the African colonies. Ghana's independence quickened the pace of British decolonisation in Africa.

globe-trotting Earl Marshal.[58] He organised the events that declared independence, birthing new states, and in so doing erasing from the British imperial map the red that signified control, one ceremony at a time.

Yet such neat formalities belied the often messy reality of events on the ground, whether in Ireland or India.[59] The partitioning of India that accompanied independence was one of the bloodiest and most devastating events of the twentieth century, impacting up to one million people on the subcontinent.[60] But partition coincided with Mountbatten's well-choreographed and publicised ceremonies, and it was these that grabbed the international headlines. Crucially, the viceroy decided not to release the details of the partition plan until after independence, in order to distance himself from the inevitable bloodshed. It has been argued that press commentary vindicated Britain for achieving a peaceful transfer of power, while at the same time British rule was supposedly vindicated by the subsequent violence that engulfed the new nation states of India and Pakistan.[61]

No such contrived public choreography happened in Dublin Castle in January 1922—at least not on the British side—and the comprehensive press coverage favoured the narrative of a 'surrender', as presented by pro-Treaty nationalists.

Endnotes

[1] NAI, TSCH 1/1/1, 17 January 1922. In the wake of increased sectarian violence and the expulsion of thousands of Catholic workers from employment in Belfast, the Dáil initiated a boycott of Belfast-manufactured goods in September 1920.

[2] Patrick McGilligan (1889–1979), academic, lawyer and politician. Left a position in University College Dublin in 1922 to become a civil servant, and that year acted as government press censor before becoming a departmental secretary. He successfully contested a by-election in November 1923 and began a career in politics, becoming minister for industry and commerce (1924–32), jointly with external affairs (1927–32) and later finance (1948–51). He was influential in discussions on the evolution of dominion status at imperial conferences in the 1920s and 1930s.

[3] NAI, TSCH 1/1/1, 17 January 1922.

[4] TNA, UK, CAB 43–6, 'Conference on Ireland with Irish ministers', 18 January 1922.

[5] NAI TSCH/3/S1. For the administrative handover of power in 1922, see McColgan, *British policy and the Irish administration*, 90–131; Maguire, *The civil service and the revolution in Ireland*, 122–69.

[6] Robinson, *Memories: wise and otherwise*, 333.

[7] Maguire, *The civil service and the revolution in Ireland*, 127.

[8] David Cannadine, 'Introduction: Independence Day ceremonials in historical perspective', *Round Table* 97 (398) (October 2008), 649–65: 652.

[9] Deirdre McMahon, 'Ireland, empire and the commonwealth', in Kevin Kenny (ed.), *Ireland and the British empire* (Oxford, 2004), 185.

[10] For overviews, see William J. Smyth, 'Nineteenth-century Ireland: transformed contexts and class structures', *Atlas of the Irish Revolution* (Cork, 2017), 4–20; Barry Crosbie, 'Ireland and the empire in the nineteenth century', in James Kelly (ed.), *Cambridge History of Ireland* vol. 3, 617–36. For contrasting conceptual assessments of Ireland's colonial status, see Stephen Howe, 'Questioning the (bad) question: "Was Ireland a colony?"', *Irish Historical Studies* 36 (142) (November 2008), 138–52; Brendan O'Leary, *A treatise on Northern Ireland,* vol. I: *Colonialism* (Oxford, 2019), 106–45.

[11] Crosbie, 'Ireland and the empire', 618.

[12] Paul A. Townend, 'Between two worlds: Irish nationalists and imperial crisis, 1878–90', *Past & Present* 194 (1) (February 2007), 139–74; Matthew Kelly, 'Irish nationalist opinion and the British empire in the 1850s and 1860s', *Past & Present* 204 (1) (August 2009), 127–54; Kate O'Malley, *Ireland, India and empire* (Manchester, 2008); Michael Silvestri, *Ireland and India: nationalism, empire and memory* (Basingstoke, 2009).

[13] Kenneth L. Shonk, 'The shadow metropole: the varieties of anticolonialism in Ireland, 1937–68', in Timothy G. McMahon, Michael De Nie and Paul Townend (eds), *Ireland in an imperial world: citizenship, opportunism and subversion* (London, 2017) 265–82.

[14] Sean Donnelly, 'Ireland in the imperial imagination: British nationalism and the Anglo-Irish Treaty', *Irish Studies Review* 27 (4) (2019), 493–511.

[15] Andrew Bonar Law (1858–1923), British Conservative politician, opponent of Irish Home Rule, prime minister (1922–3).

[16] Tom Jones (1870–1955), Welsh civil servant, deputy secretary to the British Cabinet under four prime ministers (1916–1935), described as 'keeper of a thousand secrets'. His diaries were published in three volumes (1969, 1971) and throw light on behind-the-scenes decision making in Whitehall.

[17] Thomas Jones, *Whitehall diary*, vol. III: *Ireland, 1918–1925*, ed. Keith Middlemass (Oxford, 1971), xxiii and 49–50.

[18] General Nevil Macready (1862–1946), British army officer and last British army general officer commanding in chief in Ireland (1920–2), oversaw British troop withdrawal there in 1922.

[19] CHAR 22/11, f.108, Macready to Worthington-Evans, 21 February 1922.

[20] Jones, *Whitehall diary*, 49–50.

[21] 'Dominion status' was a term used in the first half of the twentieth century to describe those colonies in the British empire that had been extensively inhabited by white settlers from the sixteenth century on, and were later granted self-government.

[22] A.G. Hopkins, 'Rethinking decolonization', *Past & Present* 200 (August 2008), 211–47. Curiously, Hopkins states in a footnote that 'there is insufficient space in this article to include Ireland, which anticipated many of the trends identified here', 212, n. 6.

[23] TNA, UK, CO 1032/406, no. 316, 'Future of remaining British dependent territories: international and strategic aspects', 6 July 1965, in, S.R. Ashton and Wm Roger Louis (eds), *East of Suez and the Commonwealth 1964–1971*, Part II: *Dependent territories, Africa, economics, race*, 283, British Documents on the End of Empire (hereafter cited as BDEEP).

[24] See Kate O'Malley, 'Ireland, India and empire: international impacts of the Irish revolutions', in John Crowley, Donal Ó Drisceoil, Mike Murphy and John Borgonovo (eds), *Atlas of the Irish Revolution* (Cork, 2017), 750–1; O'Malley, *Ireland, India and empire*.

[25] George Gavan Duffy (1882–1951), Irish politician, barrister and judge, minister for foreign affairs (January–July 1922).

[26] *DIFP I*, Doc. 221, George Gavan Duffy to John Hagan, 16 January 1922.

[27] H. Duncan Hall, *The British Commonwealth of Nations: a study of its past and future development* (London, 1920), 253–4.

[28] *DIFP I*, Doc. 250, George Gavan Duffy to Timothy A. Smiddy, 10 March 1922.

[29] Article 2 of the Treaty opens with the line: 'Subject to the provisions hereinafter set out the position of the Irish Free State in relation to the Imperial Parliament and Government and otherwise shall be that of the Dominion of Canada…'. For full text, see *DIFP I*, Doc. 214, 6 December 1921.

[30] Canadine, 'Independence Day ceremonials'.

[31] Edmund Henry Hynman Allenby, 1st Viscount Allenby (1861–1936), soldier and British imperial governor.

[32] Sa'd Zaghlul (1859–1927), Egyptian revolutionary and statesman, prime minister (January–November 1924).

[33] Kate O'Malley, 'Ireland and Egypt: anti-imperialism at bay', in Tommy Graham and Brian Hanley (eds), *History Ireland Special: A global history* (Dublin, 2019), 79–83.

[34] *Daily Mirror*, 2 March 1922.

[35] Walter Edward Guinness, 1st Baron Moyne (1880–1944), Anglo-Irish politician and businessman. British minister of state in the Middle East until November 1944, when he was assassinated.

[36] Ronald Hyam, *Britain's declining empire. The road to decolonisation 1918–68* (Cambridge, 2006), 398.

[37] Rory O'Connor (1883–1923), Irish revolutionary. The previous month, April 1922, in an act of defiance against the newly established Provisional Government, he took over the Four Courts building in Dublin with 200 anti-Treaty IRA men under his command.

[38] TNA, UK, CAB 43–6, 'Conferences on Ireland between ministers of British government and ministers of Provisional Government of Ireland, 1922', 26 May 1922.

[39] D.W. Harkness, *The restless dominion. The Irish Free State and the British Commonwealth of Nations, 1921–31* (New York, 1970), 21.

[40] John Gibney, Michael Kennedy and Kate O'Malley, *Ireland. A voice among the nations* (Dublin, 2019), 41–4.

[41] Sir Reginald Coupland (1884–1952), prominent British historian of the British empire and Beit Professor of Colonial History at the University of Oxford (1920–48).

[42] S.R. Ashton and S.E. Stockwell (eds), *Imperial policy and colonial practise 1925–45,* BDEEP, xlvii & Doc. 52 *DO* 35/398/3, no. 11111/447 [July 1933] 'An Irish fantasy': second part of a memorandum by Professor R. Coupland, 282.

[43] Malcolm MacDonald (1901–81), British politician and diplomat. Secretary of state for the dominions (1938–9), secretary of state for the colonies (1938–40), later governor-general of Kenya (1963–4).

[44] John Maynard Keynes (1883–1946), British economist and public servant.

[45] See TNA, UK, CAB 129/1, CP (45) 112, annex dated 13 August 1945, 'Our overseas financial prospects', by Lord Keynes; and Geoffrey K. Fry, *The politics of decline* (Basingstoke, 2005), 17.

[46] Chandrika Kaul, '"At the stroke of the midnight hour": Lord Mountbatten and the British media at Indian independence', *Round Table* 97 (398) (October 2008), 677–93.

[47] Louis Francis Albert Victor Nicholas Mountbatten, 1st Earl Mountbatten of Burma (1900–79), British royal navy officer, the last viceroy of India and the first governor-general of India. He was killed by the IRA while holidaying in Co. Sligo, when a bomb on his boat exploded.

[48] Kaul, '"At the stroke of the midnight hour"'.

[49] Muhammad Ali Jinnah (1876–1948), barrister, politician and founder of Pakistan.

[50] Nicholas Mansergh (ed.), *The transfer of power, 1942–47*, vol. XII (London, 1983), 770, (hereafter cited as *TOP*)

[51] Mansergh, *TOP* XII, 771.

[52] Jawaharlal Nehru (1889–1964), Indian nationalist and statesman. First prime minister of India (1947–64).

[53] Mansergh, *TOP* XII, 771–2.

[54] Mansergh, *TOP* XII, 773.

[55] Mansergh, *TOP* XII, 775.

[56] Maurice Walsh, *Bitter freedom*, 334.

[57] Sir Colin Allan (1921–1993), New Zealander who worked in the British colonial service, last governor of the Seychelles (1973–76) and of the Solomon Islands (1976–8).

[58] Cannadine, 'Independence Day ceremonials', 650–1. See also A. Faulkner, 'The man who makes a show of independence', in *Sunday Telegraph*, Magazine, 11 February 1979, 39–40.

[59] Cannadine, 'Independence Day ceremonials', 658.

[60] Kate O'Malley, '"Indian Ulsterisation"—Ireland, India and partition: the infection of example?', in Arie Dubnov and Laura Robson (eds), *Partitions: a transnational history of twentieth-century territorial separatism* (Stanford, 2019), 111–27: 111.

[61] Kaul, '"At the stroke of the midnight hour"', 691.

Chapter 4

The Castle handed over:
symbolism since 1922

THE POLICE have ORDERS
to prevent all Carts, Springvans
& Vehicles of every kind
Excepting
Gentlemen's Carriages & occupied
Hack Cars & Cabs from passing
through the Lower Castle Yard.

Dublin Castle has long been associated in the Irish mind as a symbol, of oppression—the outward sign of the system of rule against which freedom-loving Irishmen have instinctively rebelled. Castle rule, as the familiar phrase goes, was a widely-used synonym for injustice, and for the Irish people the repugnant story of Dublin Castle does not awaken pleasant memories. It was the seat of British rule in this country, and its officials were almost invariably anti-Irish in their sympathies...Dublin Castle, in a word, has long stood as a barrier to Irish freedom and progress, and it typified the rule of force which held Ireland in subjection. British Governments came and went, some professing friendliness and some openly advocating oppression, but the rule of coercion or extortion, or both, always persisted as the permanent officials at Dublin Castle remained, and Castle rule and oppression came to be regarded as interchangeable terms.[1]

The celebratory tone that accompanied the coverage of the events of 16 January 1922 in the mainstream nationalist press was not shared in all quarters. The more waspish coverage of Belfast's unionist-leaning *News-Letter* gave the impression of gross offence being given and dwelt upon the 'humiliation' inherent in such a 'deplorable' event, and the alleged insult to the viceroy, whom it claimed was kept waiting by the 'strange visitors'. These reactions are perhaps unsurprising, not least given the previous year's opening of the Belfast parliament by King George V, when pomp and pageantry abounded as the royal yacht

Previous pages: British soldiers, civilians and a police officer outside the Palace Street gate to the Lower Castle Yard, early 1922. Note the canvas screens above the gate. These were erected as a security measure to reduce visibility into the castle complex during the War of Independence, though, as can be seen, the screens had fallen into disrepair during the Truce.

arrived in Belfast Lough. 'Yesterday was a right Royal day' the *News-Letter* editorial declared on 23 June 1921:

> It was as if everyone had taken upon himself and herself to vow that nothing should occur that might tend to disturb the harmony and joy of the day...the whole day passed off with a success that was unmarred and that will leave nothing but happy memories behind it.[2]

In contrast, of the relatively lack-lustre Dublin event the following January, the *News-Letter* ominously concluded that 'The Provisional Government will have troubles and anxieties in its own area'.[3]

The Irish Times struck a subdued note, observing that the looming British withdrawal ensured that the new regime would have to secure itself from discontent. As for the use of the term 'surrender of Dublin Castle' in the official statement, according to the paper:

> The phrase contrasts ungraciously with the Lord Lieutenant's courteous language to Mr Michael Collins and his col-leagues. We may suppose, however, that these gentlemen had no desire to hurt the feelings of Irish loyalists, but have flung the word 'surrender' triumphantly at the Republicans who still refuse to admit that Ireland is free.[4]

Such commentary did not go unnoticed by the outgoing administrators. Mark Sturgis, writing in his diary on 18 January, echoed the view of *The Irish Times*, noting that

> The papers yesterday announce the 'Surrender of Dublin Castle'—the phrase used in the SF Official from the Mansion House. It leaves a nasty taste in the mouth. It is so 'caddish'. They might with advantage have confined themselves to

prompting the papers to such talk and not indulged in it 'officially'. I hope the Special Honours List will come quick—it will be the best Counter to this Surrender talk, which is galling to us, to the soldiers and the police alike, and will show that L. G. [Lloyd George] does not share this view that we are beaten.[5]

The next day he returned his focus to the incoming regime, rather than its predecessor: 'The Provisional Government are making some show of governing. I wish they would lose no time in getting the IRA into

Opposite: 21 January
1922, W.T. Cosgrave
raises the flag of
Dublin over City
Hall, which was to
become the home
of the Provisional
Government.

uniform so that all may know who's who and what's what.'[6]

Sturgis was also worried about increasing levels of robbery and violence during the interregnum ('the stealing of motors in and near Dublin is serious'). It was a valid concern. Even on the day of the handover of authority in Dublin Castle, the RIC barracks at Charlestown in Co. Mayo had been attacked by '50 armed men who captured all the arms and ammunition in the building. One Sergeant and two constables are missing'.[7] A week after the 'handover' of the Castle the British recorded that 'severe breaches' of the Truce and 'acts of lawlessness'—attacks, robberies, the kidnapping of two RIC officers in Clare, attacks on police in Kerry, and even the theft by armed men of a car belonging to FitzAlan himself—were proliferating; a sign of a 'general weakening of discipline' in the IRA following the Treaty split.[8] If power had been handed over in principle as the British withdrawal began, now it had to be handed over in practice.

On that note, attention could be directed towards the wider issues that the new administration faced, regardless of where it was located. The press carried copies of a proclamation issued by the Provisional Government confirming that it was now in charge and was prohibiting unauthorised changes in employment of state officials, and the removal or destruction of any records. Also of note was the king's telegram to the viceroy saying he was 'gratified' to hear of the government's formation.

In the meantime, the old regime continued to prepare for its departure. Sturgis, while clearing out his office and desk in Dublin Castle on 20 January, found an 'amazing collection of old letters, memoranda, SS [secret service] vouchers, etc—all thrown in anyhow and few later than 1870', in a cupboard in the official apartment of the assistant undersecretary. Given that Sturgis had arrived in Ireland as part of the planned reform of Ireland's pre-independence administration, his bemusement was perhaps to be expected:

What an amazing reflection on the long string of my distinguished predecessors as AUS that not one of them ever took the trouble or had the curiosity to turn out the contents of an open cupboard two yards from their writing table, but who could have imagined that even in Dublin Castle any papers of importance could be in such a place![9]

What next for the Castle itself? The expectations reflected in the press coverage were that the Provisional Government might soon move in, but it was also noted that the Castle was not quite handed over yet, as the lord lieutenant's apartments were still in use.[10] It was obvious that the British were a long way from physically vacating the entire complex. The *Freeman's Journal* headline had stated that 'Dublin Castle falls after seven centuries' siege', though the small print reported that the transfer of power would be restricted to 'civil' government; even though the senior civil servants had begun to contemplate the looming transition within hours of the Provisional Government's visit, the military handover would come later.[11] The *London Times* picked up on some of these points too: 'In Irish minds, the "fall of Dublin Castle" will find in Irish history a place no less prominent and unforgettable than the fall of the Bastille holds in the history of France', but noted that the inspection of the guard that had attracted so much attention from onlookers on the day was not, as was widely assumed, the last of its kind, for 'The city cannot be left undefended, and until the new Government's forces are ready British troops will continue to protect the principal city buildings.'[12] The editorial of the *New York Times* gave such sobering concerns a more breathless twist:

> Now the Castle is in Irish hands. Lord FitzAlan turns the strong place over to "Mickey" Collins. The building which meant so long English domination now stands for Irish triumph. Its possession by the Free State is one more

powerful advantage of the Provisional Government against the Irish irreconcilables. Will de Valera presently be found ranting in the old way against "Castle" influence after Michael Collins has taken up his official residence there? Not unless Irish humor is extinct. The steps already taken cannot be retraced. The abhorred Castle has now become Irish, and it is for Irishmen to make of it, if they can, the source and centre of the free and stable Government.[13]

These were themes that were amplified elsewhere. 'Dublin Castle in hands of the Irish people', proclaimed one headline in the *Evening Herald*. Its critique of the Castle and its regime, in which 'Britain gave Ireland not her best, but her absolute and unsurpassable worst', went a step further by suggesting that 'The Provisional Government will make a great mistake if it does not level Dublin Castle to the ground'.[14] Likewise the correspondent of the *Manchester Guardian* remarked that 'I hope no Irish Government will ever make it a seat of authority', for, both 'as terrible legend' and due to its more recent uses, Dublin Castle 'would be a fatal home for any Government in this country'.[15] One anonymous pro-Treaty commentator also argued that it should not take up residence in the Castle, and indeed that the place should be demolished to mark a decisive break with the past and its implications.[16] The unwelcome prospect of the lingering ghost of the Castle had already replaced the reality of Castle rule in the eyes of that particular observer.

A second handover was also reported to have taken place on 16 January, when City Hall was apparently delivered over to the town clerk, representing the corporation of Dublin. It was formally handed over to the corporation by Col. Montague Bates[17] ('commandant of the Castle') on Saturday, 21 January, and W.T. Cosgrave, as acting lord mayor, hoisted the municipal flag on a makeshift flagpole (the original flagpole had been cut down when the building was occupied in December 1920, and the British military took the flagpole they had erected with them

VIEWS OF THE MAN IN THE STREET.   16/1/22.

It seems urgently necessary that a brief statement should
be supplied officially to the Press explaining as clearly as
possible the reason for the present "duality" of Government and
the relation of the ~~European~~ Republican Cabinet and the resources to the
Provisional Government.   People generally are very much at
sea regarding this and it would be well to put the matter definitely before them in order to remove misunderstanding.

Opinion seems to be becoming more hardened in favour of
the "fait accompli" and today it was common comment that "things
appear to be getting more settled".   The temporary adjustment
of the Railway dispute caused general satisfaction.

It would be advisable for "us" to evacuate "The Castle"
as rapidly as the British.   Its complete demolition would be
desirable in order to rub into people here and everywhere that
the new Government is not going to be Castle Government in any
shape or form.   It is equally desirable that the Viceregal
Lodge should not pass to the new Governor General's hands.
It is too much identified with things that have been, and the
moral effect of severing finally these links between Great
Britain and Ireland would be tremendous.   A plain "MR"
for a Governor General would provide the anti-Treatyites with
fewer balls to fire than a titled person, and would be more
desirable on economical grounds and in fact from every point

of view. Moreover the presence of mere Misters instead of Lords and the setting of our faces against titles of all kinds would conduce to the democratisation of the country and to its more speedy "gaelicisation".

It is suggested that the Viceregal Lodge be "ear-marked" as early as possible for a Cancer Hospital. The Cancer scourge is said to be assuming exceptional proportions in Ireland and the mere fact of turning a place like the Viceregal Lodge into an Hospital would be likely to attract large subscriptions from wealthy Americans and others for its combating.

Copies to :

A. Griffith.

M. Collins.

W. Cosgrave.

K. O'Higgins.

E. O'Duffy.

R. Mulcahy.

---

when they left). It was this building rather than the Castle that would become the home of the Provisional Government, despite an unsuccessful motion being tabled a few days later by Sinn Féin councillor Kathleen Clarke,[18] demanding that the Provisional Government 'remove themselves to where they had plenty of room—namely, the Castle, that had been handed over to them'.[19]

The nascent Irish Free State had begun to paint itself, in symbolic terms, as an entity utterly distinct from the British regime it sought to supplant. If the 'Gaelic state' had, as was reported, made its first appearance in the Mansion House on 14 January, the Provisional Government repudiated the symbolism of British rule as encapsulated by the Castle as a seat of government by declining to use it. Dublin City Council had long been a body reflective of nationalist civil society in the capital; its premises were perhaps a more natural home for the new government.[20]

There were, however, good practical reasons why the government might base itself in City Hall. Dublin Castle may have been the scene of the transfer of authority to the Provisional Government on 16 January 1922, but contrary to what readers of the next day's papers might have assumed, the premises themselves were not actually handed over. In mid-February representatives of Dublin Corporation visited the Castle to determine whether they could make use of some of the buildings, only to find that the British evacuation was proceeding much more slowly than was expected. Some civil servants such as Alfred Cope[21] were still in situ even at the end of February, in order to liaise with the new government.[22] As late as 11 March FitzAlan attended an organ recital in the Chapel Royal and members of the British forces still present in

Previous pages: Some thoughts on the handing over of the Castle and its future, seemingly from a source close to the pro-Treaty leadership. The suggestion that the viceregal lodge could become a cancer hospital was met with great hostility by the British when it was later repeated by Michael Collins.

Opposite: A pro-Treaty poster listing sixteen points in support of the Treaty. Note the green text toward the end declaring 'DUBLIN CASTLE HAS FALLEN!'

THE TREATY
GIVES IRELAND

1. A PARLIAMENT RESPONSIBLE TO THE IRISH PEOPLE ALONE.

2. A GOVERNMENT RESPONSIBLE TO THAT PARLIAMENT.

3. DEMOCRATIC CONTROL OF ALL LEGISLATIVE AFFAIRS.

4. POWER TO MAKE LAWS FOR EVERY DEPARTMENT OF IRISH LIFE.

5. AN IRISH LEGAL SYSTEM CONTROLLED BY IRISHMEN.

6. AN IRISH ARMY.

7. AN IRISH POLICE FORCE.

8. COMPLETE FINANCIAL FREEDOM.

9. A NATIONAL FLAG.

10. FREEDOM OF OPINION.

11. COMPLETE CONTROL OF IRISH EDUCATION.

12. COMPLETE CONTROL OF HER LAND SYSTEMS.

13. POWER AND FREEDOM TO DEVELOP HER RESOURCES AND INDUSTRIES.

14. A DEMOCRATIC CONSTITUTION.

15. A STATE ORGANISATION TO EXPRESS THE MIND AND WILL OF THE NATION.

16. HER RIGHTFUL PLACE AS A NATION AMONG NATIONS.

DUBLIN CASTLE HAS FALLEN !
BRITISH BUREAUCRACY IS IN THE DUST !
IS THIS VICTORY OR DEFEAT ?

SUPPORT THE TREATY

British troops march past the train depot (later the Point Depot) en route to Dublin's North Wall, as British forces withdrew from the territory of the future Irish Free State.

the Castle marked St Patrick's Day (some sections of the complex, such as the chapel and state apartments, were apparently still reserved for his usage).[23] At the end of March, even MPs in Westminster seemed bemused that British officials were still based in Dublin Castle, given that it had supposedly been taken over by the Provisional Government.[24] It was not until early May that Greenwood could publicly confirm that all departments bar those of the chief

Troops buying fruit prior to their departure from Dublin, while seemingly trying their charm on the local vendors.

Following pages: Troops of the newly established National Army march over the Shannon Road Bridge in Athlone, to take over Victoria (later Custume) Barracks on 25 February 1922. By this time all British troops west of the Shannon had been withdrawn from Ireland.

secretary and the inspector general of the RIC had been transferred to the Provisional Government, that no military remained in Dublin Castle, and that it was the RIC who now occupied Ship Street Barracks and provided the Castle guard.[25] The British military withdrawal from Ireland was, by now, nearing its end and a new Irish administration was populating the Castle.

The Castle had been regularly name-checked in reportage and political discourse in Ireland and overseas since January. One report on the Irish Race Convention being held in Paris that spring made an inevitable (and oft-repeated) comparison with the Bastille.[26] Towards the end of February it was reported that Collins had been congratulated by the 'Tradesmen's Help League, Lwow (Lemburg), Cracow Branch', and this gesture of Polish solidarity explicitly offered 'our most enthusiastic congratulations on the occasion

Opposite: Extract from minutes of a meeting of the Provisional Government, 2 August 1922, entitled 'Taking over of the Castle', detailing an upcoming meeting with Alfred Cope to arrange the 'final taking over of the Castle by the Provisional Government'.

of your entry into possession of Dublin Castle, which for 700 years was the stronghold of foreign tyranny in Ireland'.[27] The ostensible handing over or surrendering of the Castle was also a point of reference for MPs in Westminster who were skeptical of the intentions of the Provisional Government; after all, as one MP put it on 31 May, 'We have handed over Dublin Castle and all that it stands for.'[28] In Ireland, the strength of the subliminal significance attached to the very word 'castle' remained, with both sides of the Treaty split claiming their opponents had adopted the 'methods' of the 'castle', and even the Labour Party, prior to the June general election, declared it 'would not tolerate the continuance under an Irish ministry of the Dublin Castle system'.[29]

Reality resurfaced amidst the symbolism in August 1922, after the outbreak of the civil war, when the Provisional Government began to make arrangements for the 'final acquisition' of the Castle.[30] It was supposed to have taken possession on 15 August, but the proceedings were rescheduled for 17 August due to the security situation and the funeral of Arthur Griffith, which had proceeded from City Hall to Glasnevin Cemetery on the previous day.[31] There were 80 members of the RIC still in the complex on the day of the 'final evacuation', and some of the British troops still stationed in Dublin (a detachment of the King's Shropshire Light Infantry) were sent from Richmond Barracks to relieve

RIALTAS SEALADACH NA HÉIREANN
(IRISH PROVISIONAL GOVERNMENT)

Reference No.

S.................................

BAILE ÁTHA CLIATH.

MEETING OF THE PROVISIONAL GOVERNMENT

HELD ON THE   2nd August,   1922.

P.G.80.

TO:
Acting Chairman.

The following extract from the Minutes of the
above Meeting ~~are~~ is sent you for your information.

A letter was sent in this connection to the Commander-
in-Chief. on the 3rd inst.

Gniomh Runai Co'n Rialtas.

4th August,1922.

EXTRACT.
--------   TAKING OVER OF THE CASTLE: It was decided
that the Acting Chairman should see the Commander-in-Chief
and Mr. Cope with a view to arranging for the final taking
over of the Castle by the Provisional Government.

the RIC who had been on guard. They took over at 8 a.m., and the RIC began to prepare for their final departure not just from the Castle, but from Irish life: 'kits, caps, uniforms, and all the discarded paraphernalia of the one-time semi-military force strewed the ground. So it was until the early afternoon, when all the "packing" had been accomplished.'[32] In the meantime crowds had gathered outside the gate to the Lower Yard from 11.30 a.m., and at 1.30 p.m. 380 members of the new Civic Guard

The first detachment of the Civic Guards (later An Garda Síochána) entering Dublin Castle, led by Chief Superintendent McCarthy (left) and Commissioner Michael Staines on 17 August 1922. A small crowd lines the route and looks on. Staines was the first Garda Commissioner. They are entering through the Palace Street gate. Two soldiers stand on the left, with an impromptu gathering of members of the public on the right.

arrived at the Castle, having paraded through the city following their arrival by train from Newbridge, Co. Kildare. Those who were to take over guard duties armed themselves at Ship Street Barracks before relieving the last guard of British soldiers at 2.40 p.m. While General Macready described them as 'a fine body of men' with 'a smart blue uniform', the British officer in charge, Major L.H. Torin, hinted at an undercurrent of tension: 'No compliments were paid by the guards of my detachment to the relieving guards'. He, along with the soldiers under his command, departed at 3.15 p.m., 'The tricolour was hoisted over the main gate as my convoy left the Castle.'[33]

That was finally that. As George C. Duggan had put it in his account of the last years of British rule, published less than a fortnight earlier

> Dublin Castle's day is over. It now exists but as a name—Castle rule—a symbol of government without the consent of the governed; but in its time it did govern: it accomplished its purpose, though that purpose was often narrow, ill-advised, and, above all, unimaginative. In the mouth of the Irish peasant it was a synonym for repression, but the peasant had broken its power twenty years before its end came. Yet the tradition is such that the Government of the Free State has hesitated to set up within its walls even the least of its Departments. It fears the taint that still clings to the name.
>
> To-day in its all but deserted rooms the dust is beginning to gather; the silence comes oppressive. One feels that in spite of all the curses that were heaped upon it by a nation, in spite of the wrongs it did, the evils that it condoned, here was something which lived, and now the life has gone from it.[34]

Earlier in the year there had been just enough space left on the panels of the Chapel Royal to insert the coats of arms of the last four viceroys.[35]

Uniforms can be seen dumped outside Ship Street Barracks within Dublin Castle, during its final evacuation by the RIC, on 17 August 1922. People are leaving the area carrying boxes and belongings, and the girl in the white dress is wearing a discarded beret.

Yet such a neat symbolic closure was not to be reflected by realities on the ground. The perceived and potential abandonment of a large population of loyal subjects in the wake of a British withdrawal had been a running theme in the background of Treaty negotiations, and the day after the handing over of the Castle a letter appeared in the press announcing a meeting that was to take place on the afternoon of Thursday, 19 January. Arranged by the Earl of Mayo, it was to propose a resolution that the Unionists of the South and West of Ireland, recognising that a Provisional Government has been formed, desire to co-operate with our fellow-countrymen in this Government, in order that peace may be brought about, and the welfare of the community secured.[36]

Following pages: National Army troops in an armoured car outside the Cork Hill Gate of Dublin Castle, 1922. Van Nost's 1753 statue of Justice is seen above the gate in the right corner facing inwards; the *Freeman's Journal's* report on the 'handover', published on 17 January 1922, observed that 'It was noticed by many for the first time that Justice is represented with her back to the city'.

Given the speed with which it appeared, its authors presumably had taken an interest in what had happened in Dublin Castle the previous day, but their desire to reach an accommodation with the new regime was tempered by an accompanying letter to Lord Mayo from the Unionist Anti-Partition League, expressing the view that 'it would be most unwise to hold a public meeting of Southern Unionists at the present time'. The fears of a minority about life under a new regime ran through both letters.

What now for Dublin Castle in an independent Ireland? After 1922 various plans were put forward for the symbolic reworking of Dublin's post-independence streetscape, some of which were grandiose but all of which came to nothing, primarily on grounds of cost. There was little room for the Georgian city in the conception of the new state, and especially for the former seat of British rule.[37]

The Castle was briefly considered as the seat of the Irish government prior to Leinster House assuming that role on a permanent basis, but the idea was not pursued. Speaking in the Dáil in 1924, Labour TD William Davin noted that 'Dublin Castle has many historical associations which would not commend it to us for that particular purpose', to which Denis Gorey of the Farmers' Party responded:

(2184) M.1561. Wt.957. D.45. 3,000—6-35—F.P.—G.24.
(2667) M.8602. Wt.4327. D.89. 3,000. 1-36.—F.P.—G.24.

ROINN AN UACHTARÁIN

Sgeul, ... Provisional Government 1922 ....

....

Article 17 of the Treaty between Great
Britain and Ireland, dated 6th December, 1921,
provided that every member of the Irish Provisional
Government should signify in writing his or her
acceptance of the Treaty.

A minute of a meeting of the Provisional
Government of 13th August, 1922, (reference P.G.104)
records that every member of that Government named
therein had already signified in writing his acceptance
of the Treaty.

I cannot, however, trace the actual signed
documents.   On the 19th September, 1922, I wrote
to Mr. Cope, representative of the British Government,
asking him whether any written notification had been
sent to the British Govt. from here regarding the
Constitution and personnel of the Provisional
Government as originally formed.   He did not reply
in writing but informed Miss Sheila Murphy of the
Secretariat that no such notification had been sent
but that on the occasion of the taking over of Dublin
Castle on the 16th January, 1922, each member of the
Provisional Government had verbally signified his
acceptance of the Treaty.

Opposite: An undated
minute detailing that the
written records relating to
the handover of Dublin
Castle in January 1922
had, by September 1922,
gone missing, if indeed
they had ever existed;
Alfred Cope confirms
that the acceptance of the
Treaty by the Provisional
Government was
confirmed verbally rather
than in writing. Sheila
Murphy, referred to here,
enjoyed a long career as a
senior official and diplomat
in the Department of
External Affairs.

Deputy Davin talks about the associations of Dublin Castle and what it stood
for in the past. I am not concerned at
all for what Dublin Castle stood for in
the past. What does it stand for now?
What did it stand for two or three years
ago when General Collins took it over?
It did not stand for the past. Dublin
Castle stands for the present; it stands
for victory; it stands for triumph.[38]

There were genuine grounds on which to rec-
ommend its use—its location, size, and the
fact that it was ready to use—but there were
also practical objections: the Castle had been
adapted as a temporary home for the courts of
justice until the Four Courts, destroyed in the civil war, were rebuilt.
In the plans of the 'Greater Dublin Reconstruction Movement' of the
1920s it was suggested that Dublin Castle could remain as the home
of the courts, making it little more than a stop on a proposed 'national
highway' ending at new parliament buildings beside the Royal Hospital
Kilmainham.[39] As the restoration of the Four Courts neared completion
The Irish Times asked

> What will become of Dublin Castle? Will it again become
> the official residence of the Governor-General, the present
> representative of the King in Ireland? It is generally believed
> that this is the intention of the Irish Free State Government.[40]

After the courts officially returned across the River Liffey to the Four
Courts in October 1931 it remained unclear what role the newly vacated
Castle would have, though suggestions that it could be made use of for

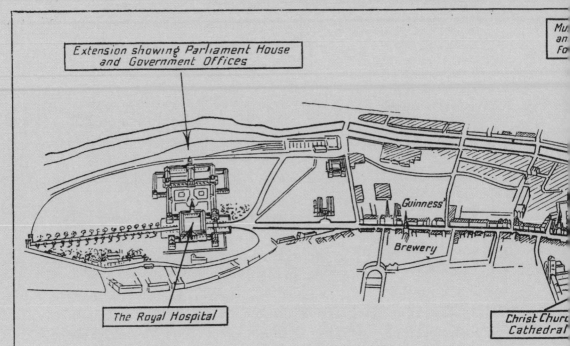

Extension showing Parliament House
and Government Offices

Mu
an
Fo

Guinness'

Brewery

The Royal Hospital

Christ Churc
Cathedral

the Eucharistic Congress the following year were dismissed.[41] A change of government brought a change of plan, however, and on 24 June 1932 the Fianna Fáil government of Éamon de Valera hosted a reception in the Castle for the papal legate, Cardinal Lorenzo Lauri, on the eve of the opening of the Eucharistic Congress. It was even redecorated for the occasion.[42] The reception was attended by a wide range of dignitaries—diplomatic, political and ecclesiastical— but, as *The Irish Times* reported, 'it was a gathering which suffered from

Throughout the 1920s, while the Four Courts was being rebuilt after the civil war, Dublin Castle served as the home for the 'courts of justice'. This map, from the Greater Dublin Reconstruction Movement in 1922, proposed the Castle as the courts' new permanent home.

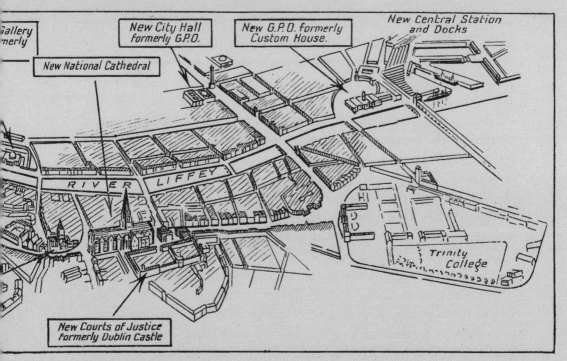

Labels on map: Gallery merly / New National Cathedral / New City Hall formerly G.P.O. / New G.P.O. formerly Custom House. / New Central Station and Docks / RIVER LIFFEY / Trinity College / New Courts of Justice Formerly Dublin Castle

only one unfortunate omission. That was the absence of Mr McNeill, the Free State Governor-General, who had not been invited'.[43] In both the reception and this omission were the shape of things to come.

This new role for the Castle as a ceremonial centre in independent Ireland was confirmed the following year. The State Apartments and St Patrick's Hall had been renovated by March 1933, in time to host another reception on St Patrick's Day, apparently for 'the purpose of giving the members of the Diplomatic and Consular Corps in the Free State an opportunity of making the acquaintance of the members of the executive council and the members of the Senate and Dáil'.[44] There was no mention of the governor-general, presaging the eventual breaking of the final links between Ireland and the empire, and the consequent redundancy of the Castle as a potential symbol of such a link in the future. In that sense, here was a decisive break with the past.

In the decades after its evacuation by the British the Castle remained an administrative centre, and it has since hosted myriad official events. There has been a certain continuity of purpose in that regard, but the Castle has never since been a seat of executive power. Having been vacated by the British, in many ways the Castle faded into the background of Irish life, and one might argue that its symbolism was reclaimed: instead of housing a government headed by a viceroy, Dublin Castle has, since the 1930s, hosted the inaugurations of the presidents of an independent Irish state. Over time 'Leinster House' has replaced 'Dublin Castle' as a synonym for the government of Ireland, albeit in very different hands.

Yet it is strange that the Castle did not become a site of commemoration for the final event in which it played such a crucial role; a site of 'historical remembrance', as Jay Winter would put it, relating to the British withdrawal.[45] After all, other commemorations relating to the independence struggle took place within its walls: memorial masses for Peadar Clancy and Dick McKee, and even for Michael Collins himself, which took place in the Church of the Most Holy Trinity, formerly the Chapel Royal. These were not necessarily organised by the state, but they were sometimes attended by leading politicians from both sides of the civil war divide: masses for Collins were attended by W.T. Cosgrave as late as 1965, the year of his death, and finally by de Valera himself in 1968.[46] In 1997 An Garda Síochána staged an event to mark the 75th anniversary of their forebears marching into the Castle in August 1922.[47] Nevertheless, the symbolic power of the handover, or surrender, or fall, of Dublin Castle in 1922 did not get the traction accorded other events in the revolution.

The handover on 16 January 1922 was associated with, and perhaps overshadowed by, the civil war that followed, and by the fact that loss became such a potent focal point for the remembrance of the war.[48] For the veterans and political descendants of the pro-Treaty side there were, perhaps other, *better* dates and *clearer-cut* events to focus on, such as the deaths of fallen leaders like Griffith and Collins. It was also, presumably, an unappealing event for the descendants of the anti-Treaty camp to dwell upon, and they were, after all, in power for so much of the twentieth century. The ghost of Dublin Castle had been exorcised from Ireland's political landscape and the Castle itself seems to have fallen through the cracks.

All of which begs the question what actually happened in Dublin Castle on 16 January 1922, and what might have been commemorated had anyone thought it prudent to do so? One might, in hindsight, expect a ceremony, but the events had been marked with little in the way of ceremony at the time. The late-Victorian and the Edwardian era witnessed a 'general proliferation of new or revived ceremonial during this period, which characterised English, European and American public life, not only at the level of the head of state, but in a more widespread manner as well'.[49] Such ceremonials in the United Kingdom, and across the empire and its dominions, were geared toward asserting and strengthening power and formalising continued links, however; not ushering in its decline and demise. A ceremonial template would evolve as the British withdrew from 'dependent territories' across the world in the decades that followed, as we have seen, and the image of the handing over of Dublin Castle, as occasionally name-checked in the press over the years, slotted into a rhetorical template in which flags came down and keys were handed over.[50]

The last word on the events of 16 January 1922 as reported are sometimes left to *The Irish Times*, in an oft-quoted passage that sums up the understated reality of what happened:

> After the fluctuating history of seven centuries Dublin Castle is no longer the fortress of British power in Ireland. Having withstood the attacks of successive generations of rebels, it was quietly handed over yesterday to eight gentlemen in three taxi-cabs.[51]

The low-key nature of the occasion was touched upon in reports of the taking over of barracks across Ireland as the British military departed, some of which were deemed equally mundane, or more impressive.[52] Despite the ways in which the 'handing over' of Dublin Castle was reported in the press, it was essentially a routine affair, a date in a diary as opposed to an 'event'. On Saturday, 14 January 1922, Michael Collins had seemed to view what was a procedural meeting with the viceroy to confirm the authority of the government he was to lead as being sufficiently unimportant to not be worth attending. Things had changed by Monday, and Mark Sturgis may have had a point when he suspected that the newspapers had been well briefed by the incoming Provisional Government. The press in West Cork, however, essentially summed up the essence of what had taken place when the *Skibbereen Eagle*, reporting on the handover a few days after it happened, explicitly stated that FitzAlan received the new ministers as 'a Privy Council'.[53] This seems to have been at the core of what happened on 16 January, but as one official noted the following June, 'The handing over of Dublin Castle to the Provisional Government was done in an informal manner and I am not aware of any official document relating to the transaction.'[54]

International news coverage was more sanguine than its Irish counterparts; were the Irish papers subjected to 'spinning' by the pro-Treaty side to emphasise the symbolism of the event, as Mark Sturgis had suspected? The Provisional Government's statement on the 'surrender' was not an agreed document, and there were reports that the precise details of what would happen in Dublin Castle remained unclear until the eleventh hour. Did the members of the newly appointed government simply go to the Castle to confirm their role and relationship with the viceroy, and was the meeting then used to gain some good symbolic publicity? This was unfamiliar territory for the British, who may have placed more faith in Greenwood's observation that the withdrawal of the military would be the most visible signifier that they were leaving. This perhaps indicates that, from the British perspective, 16 January 1922 was a procedural sideshow. Kevin O'Higgins later downplayed its significance when he described the event as 'that little scene and ceremony in the Castle when eight of us were greeted by the man who was Lord Lieutenant of Ireland', and he had prefaced his description by stating that

> When we went to Dublin Castle—eight of us—and were greeted there by Lord FitzAlan, in the presence of the heads of the Civil Service, as the Government of Ireland it was not as the Provisional Government. It was not that greeting that made us the Provisional Government. It was the facts arising from the Treaty, and it was certain facts that had been going on here for some years before, that gave rise to that Treaty.[55]

Nevertheless, symbols count for a great deal, and clarity surrounding the events of the day was not required by those whose jubilation was silently recorded by cameramen, or who read about it in newspapers, or had heard about it from friends and acquaintances, and presumably discussed it in venues scattered across a city that was taking stock during the strange respite between wars. Their experience of that day, and their reactions to what had happened, remain elusive, but a fragment can be found in the recollection of Collins's comrade Batt O'Connor, long before he published his memoirs. Writing to his sister less than a fortnight after the event, O'Connor left a vivid impression of what he had seen in Dublin Castle on 16 January 1922 and the emotions it evoked, at least in him:

Following pages: An engraving from 1879 of the Chapel Royal, which was the official chapel of the household of the lord lieutenant of Ireland from 1814 until the creation of the Irish Free State in December 1922. The Chapel itself is adorned with the coats of arms of the viceroys, and, fortuitously, the very last space came to be occupied by the arms of the very last viceroy. It was reconsecrated as a garrison chapel for the Irish Defence Forces in 1943 (with some observers noting the contrast with its former role). In 1944 the Chapel was renamed as the Church of the Most Holy Trinity and, amongst other events, hosted commemorative masses for figures such as Michael Collins, Peadar Clancy and Dick McKee. It closed for renovations in 1983 but was not used for worship thereafter.

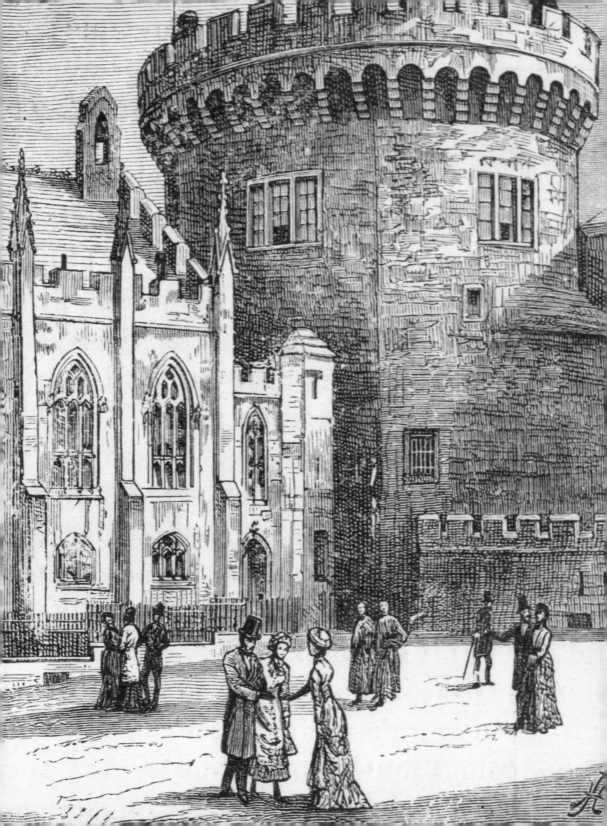

Well I witnessed the greatest event in all my life the day I stood among a crowd of sightseers at Dublin Castle and beheld Michael Collins accompanied by his other ministers drive in to the Upper Castle Yard in their swell auto's [*sic.*] to take the surrender of Dublin Castle. I wonder can you picture my feelings of joy & gratification in seeing the man above all others who laid the plans to break the power of this same castle, politely walk in and take over its power and all it stood for. No matter what ever may become of me now, and no matter what I have risked and suffered…I am repaid a thousand times over to witness what I saw taking place that never to be forgotten day at Dublin Castle.[56]

The day itself may have been overlooked by posterity; for some contemporaries, however, it was clear what they felt they had witnessed. The Castle had fallen.

Opposite: Batt O'Connor's account of the handover of Dublin Castle, as written to his sister Máire, 28 January 1922.

but. I had to choose between my Country and a man, and I have put my country first. And I tell you I found it hard to take sides against such a charming personality as brave De Valera My Conscience would upraid me to plunge our people into bloodshed + slaughter; and knowing so well how few of us had to carry on the fight. here in Dublin for the past few years, I also knew if the fight started again we would be beaten hopelessly + the whole country + the whole world (including America) would blame us for refusing such generous terms as this Treaty offered. England would (have) gained the ear of the world when she would tell broadcast the terms she offered. and I am sure many who now are saying hard things against us in America, would say we were fools that did not take the terms + give the country a chance to get on its feet + then look for the complete thing when the occasion offered.   Well I witnessed the greatest. event. in all my life the day I stood amongst a crowd of sightseers at. Dublin Castle and beheld Michael Collins accompanied by his other Ministers drive in to the Upper Castle yard in their swell Autos to take the Surrender of Dublin Castle I wonder Can you picture my feelings. Joy + gratification in seeing the man above all others who laid the plans to break the power of this same castle, politely walk in and take over all its power and all it. stood for. No matter what. ever may become of me now. and no matter what. I have risked and suffered (and I have lost. heavy financially in the struggle) I am repaid a thousand times over. to witness what I saw taking place that. never to be forgotten day at. Dublin Castle, As Michael

Endnotes

[1] *Cork Examiner*, 17 January 1922.

[2] *Belfast News-Letter*, 23 June 1921.

[3] *Belfast News-Letter*, 17 January 1922.

[4] *The Irish Times*, 17 January 1922.

[5] Sturgis, *Diaries*, 227.

[6] Sturgis, *Diaries*, 227–8.

[7] TNA, UK, CAB 24–132–56, 'Report by General Officer Commanding-in-Chief on the situation in Ireland for week ending 21st January, 1922'.

[8] TNA, UK, CAB 24–132–38, 'Weekly survey of the state of Ireland', 20 January 1922; CAB 24–132–58, 'Weekly survey of the state of Ireland', 23 January 1922.

[9] Sturgis, *Diaries*, 228.

[10] *The Irish Times*, 17 January 1922.

[11] Brendan O'Donoghue, *Activities wise and otherwise: the career of Sir Henry Augustus Robinson, 1898–1922* (Sallins, 2015), 393–4.

[12] *London Times*, 17 January 1922.

[13] *New York Times*, 17 January 1922.

[14] *Evening Herald*, 16 January 1922.

[15] *Manchester Guardian*, 17 January 1922.

[16] NAI, TSHC/3/S26. This suggestion that the Viceregal Lodge would make a good cancer hospital arose again on 26 February 1922, during a meeting in London in which the status of the royal representative was discussed. Arthur Griffith was reminded by Austen Chamberlain 'of a remark which Mr Collins had made to the effect that the Vice-Regal Lodge would make an admirable cancer hospital'. When Griffith dismissed this as a joke, Chamberlain replied that 'jokes were so dangerous. The question was one of the greatest importance to HM Government who could not consent to the humiliation of the Representative of the Crown': TNA, UK, CAB 43–6 (74), 'Conference on Ireland with Irish ministers', 26 February 1922.

[17] Lieutenant-Colonel Francis Stewart 'Frank' Montague-Bates (1876–1954), British army officer appointed officer commanding troops at Dublin Castle in June 1921.

[18] Kathleen Clarke (1878–1972), Irish revolutionary, founder member of Cumann na mBan. Wife of Thomas Clarke and sister of Edward Daly, both men were executed in the wake of the Easter Rising. She was subsequently alderman, TD, senator and the first female lord mayor of Dublin (1939–41).

[19] *Manchester Guardian*, 17 January 1922; *Freeman's Journal*, 23, 26 January 1922; *Belfast News-Letter,* 23 January 1922.

[20] Ciarán Wallace, 'Civil society in search of a state: Dublin 1898–1922', *Urban History* 45 (3) (2017), 426–52.

[21] Sir Alfred 'Andy' William Cope (1877–1954), British civil servant, assistant under-secretary for Ireland (1920–22).

[22] *Freeman's Journal*, 17 February 1922. TNA, UK, CAB 24–133–100, 'Report by General Officer Commanding-in-Chief on the situation in Ireland for week ending 28th February, 1922'.

[23] *Freeman's Journal*, 11 March 1922; *Irish Independent*, 18 March 1922; *The Irish Times*, 17 January 1922; TNA, UK, CO 904/180.

[24] *Hansard*, HC, vol. 152, col. 1513, 30 March 1922.

[25] *Irish Independent*, 5 May 1922, 10 May 1922.

[26] *Irish Independent*, 26 January 1922.

[27] *Freeman's Journal*, 27 February1922.

[28] *Hansard*, HC, vol. 154, col. 2159, 31 May 1922. See also, vol. 150, col. 2190, 23 February 1922.

[29] *Irish Independent*, 7 April 1922; *Freeman's Journal*, 21 July 1922; 9 June 1922.

[30] NAI, TSCH/3/S2159.

[31] TNA, UK, CAB 24–138–66, 'Report on the situation in Ireland for the week ending 12th August, 1922'.

[32] *Irish Independent*, 18 August 1922.

[33] TNA, UK, CAB 24–138–72, 'Report on the situation in Ireland for the week ending 19th August, 1922'. The *Irish Independent* on 18 August 1922, reported that the flag was 'displayed from one of the upper windows in the Lower Castle Yard'.

[34] Duggan, 'Last days', 189–90.

[35] *Irish Independent*, 11 March 1922.

[36] *Freeman's Journal, Irish Independent*, 17 January 1922.

[37] Mary Daly, 'Dublin: the restored capital', in Howard Clarke, Jacinta Prunty and Mark Hennessy (eds), *Surveying Ireland's past* (Dublin, 2004), 565–83.

[38] *Dáil debates*, vol. 8, no. 9, 'Temporary accommodation of the Oireachtas', 10 July 1924.

[39] Yvonne Whelan, '"Written in space and stone": aspects of the iconography of Dublin after independence', in Clarke *et al.* (eds), *Surveying*, 585–612.

[40] *Weekly Irish Times*, 6 December 1930.

[41] *The Irish Times*, 1 October 1931.

[42] *Dáil debates*, vol. 44, no. 9, 'Vote No. 66–External Affairs', 4 November 1932.

[43] *Weekly Irish Times*, 25 June 1932.

[44] *The Irish Times*, 14 March 1933.

[45] Jay Winter, 'Sites of memory', in Susannah Radstone and Bill Schwarz (eds), *Memory: histories, theories, debates* (New York, 2010), 312–24.

[46] *Irish Press*, 21 June 1965; *Irish Independent*, 5 July 1968.

[47] *Irish Independent*, 18 August 1997.

[48] This is a central theme in Anne Dolan, *Commemorating the Irish civil war: history and memory, 1923–2000* (Cambridge, 2003).

[49] David Cannadine, 'The context, performance and meaning of ritual: the British monarchy and the "Invention of tradition", *c.*1820–1977', in Eric Hobsbawm and Terence Ranger (eds), *The invention of tradition* (Cambridge, 1983), 101–64: 138. See also Bernard S. Cohn, 'Representing authority in Victorian India', Hobsbawm and Ranger (eds), *The invention of tradition*, 165–209.

[50] *Irish Press*, 16 January 1989; *Irish Examiner*, 28 April 1990. See Guy Beiner, 'Probing the boundaries of Irish memory: from postmemory to prememory and back', *Irish Historical Studies* 39 (154) (November 2014), 296–307.

[51] *The Irish Times*, 17 January 1922

[52] *Freeman's Journal*, 17 May 1922

[53] *Skibbereen Eagle*, 21 January 1922

[54] TNA, UK, CO 904/180.

[55] *Dáil debates*, 'The Dáil in committee—Article 79', 11 October 1922.

[56] UCDA, P68/4 (2), Batt O'Connor to Máire O'Connor, 28 January 1922.

GOOD BYE

Abbreviations

BMH	Military Archives, Bureau of Military History
DCLA	Dublin City Library and Archives
DMP	Dublin Metropolitan Police
IRA	Irish Republican Army
NAI	National Archives, Ireland
NGI	National Gallery of Ireland
NLI	National Library of Ireland
OPW	Office of Public Works
RIC	Royal Irish Constabulary
RTÉ	Raidió Teilifís Éireann
TD	Teachta Dála, elected member of Dáil Éireann
TNA, UK	The National Archives, United Kingdom
UCDA	University College Dublin Archives
UN	United Nations

Previous pages: British troops mark their impending departure from Dublin, 1922. The soldier writing the inscription, Christopher Aiken, was from Belfast.

Select bibliography

Andrews, C.S., 2001 *Dublin made me*. Dublin. Lilliput Press.

Brady, Joseph and Anngret Simms (eds), 2001 *Dublin through space and time*. Dublin. Four Courts.

Brown, Terence, 1985 *Ireland: a social and cultural history 1922–85*. London. Fontana.

Campbell, Myles and William Derham (eds), 2015 *The Chapel Royal Dublin Castle: an architectural history*. Dublin. OPW.

Cannadine, David, 2008 'Introduction: Independence Day ceremonials in historical perspective', *Round Table*, 97, (398) (October), 649–65.

Casey, Christine, 2005 *Dublin: the city within the Grand and Royal Canals and the Circular Road with the Phoenix Park*. New Haven,CT. Yale University Press.

Clarke, Howard, Jacinta Prunty and Mark Hennessy (eds), 2004 *Surveying Ireland's past*. Dublin. Geography Publications.

Crowley, John, Donal Ó Drisceoil and Mike Murphy (eds), John Borgonovo (associate ed.), 2017 *Atlas of the Irish Revolution*. Cork. Cork University Press.

d'Alton, Ian and Ida Milne (eds), 2019 *Protestant and Irish: the minority's search for place in independent Ireland* Cork. Cork University Press.

Delaney, Enda and Fearghal McGarry, 2020 'Introduction: a global history of the Irish revolution', *Irish Historical Studies* 44 (165), 1–10.

Dickson, David, 2014 *Dublin: the making of a capital*. London. Profile Books.

Dolan, Anne, 2003 *Commemorating the Irish civil war: history and memory, 1923–2000*. Cambridge. Cambridge University Press.

Dolan, Anne and William Murphy, 2018 *Michael Collins. The man and the revolution*. Dublin. Collins Press.

Fanning, Ronan, 2013 *Fatal path: British government and Irish revolution, 1910–1922*. London.). Faber and Faber.

Fenlon, Jane, 2017 *Dublin Castle guidebook*. Dublin. OPW.

Gibney, John, 2017 *A short history of Ireland, 1500–2000*. New Haven, CT. Yale University Press.

Gibney, John, 2018 *Revolution and civil war in Dublin, 1918–1923: an illustrated history*. Cork. Collins Press.

Gray, Peter and Olwen Purdue (eds), 2012 *The Irish lord lieutenancy, c. 1541–1922*. Dublin. UCD Press.

Harkness, D.W., 1970 *The restless dominion: the Irish Free State and the British Commonwealth of Nations, 1921–31*. New York. New York University Press.

Hopkinson, Michael, 1988 *Green against green: the Irish civil war*. Dublin. Gill and Macmillan.

Hopkinson, Michael, 2002 *The Irish war of independence*. Dublin. Gill Books.

Hyam, Ronald, 2006 *Britain's declining empire: the road to decolonisation 1918–68*. Cambridge. Cambridge University Press.

Kenny, Kevin (ed.), 2004 *Ireland and the British empire*. Oxford. Oxford University Press.

Kinsella, Alan, 1998 '"Goodbye Dublin": the British military evacuation 1922', *Dublin Historical Record* 51 (1) (Spring), 4–24.

McColgan, John, 1983 *British policy and the Irish administration, 1920–22*. London. Allen and Unwin.

Maguire, Martin, 2008 *The civil service and the revolution in Ireland,1912–38: 'Shaking the blood-stained hand of Mr Collins'*. Manchester. Manchester University Press.

Ó Broin, Leon (ed.), 1996 *In great haste: the letters of Michael Collins and Kitty Kiernan*. Dublin. Gill and Macmillan.

O'Halpin, Eunan, 1987 *The decline of the union: British government in Ireland, 1898–1921*. Dublin and Syracuse, NY. Gill and Macmillan and Syracuse University Press.

O'Malley, Ernie, 1961 *On another man's wound*. London. Four Square Books.

O'Malley, Kate, 2007 *Ireland, India and empire: Indo-Irish radical connections, 1919–1964*. Manchester. Manchester University Press.

Ó Ruairc, Padraig Óg, 2011 *Revolution: a photographic history of revolutionary Ireland, 1913–23*. Cork. Mercier Press.

'Periscope' [G.C. Duggan], 1922 'The last days of Dublin Castle', *Blackwoods Magazine* 212 (1282) August, 137–90.

Robinson, Henry, 1923 *Memories: wise and otherwise*. London. Cassell and Company.

Townshend, Charles, 2012 *The Republic: the fight for Irish independence, 1918–23*. London. Allen Lane.

Walsh, Maurice, 2015 *Bitter freedom: Ireland in a revolutionary world, 1918–1923*. London. Faber and Faber.

Yeates, Padraig, 2013 *A city in turmoil: Dublin, 1919–21*. Dublin. Gill and Macmillan.

Yeates, Padraig, 2015 *A city in civil war: Dublin, 1921–23*. Dublin. Gill and Macmillan.

Image credits

Frontispiece Alamy; Smith Archive/Alamy, 2BWFHP6; reproduced courtesy of Alamy.

p. vi NLI, Irish Newspaper Archive, *Evening Herald*, 16 January 1922; courtesy of the National Library of Ireland.

pp x–xi Irish Architectural Archive, Photographic collections, 9/15Yy1; courtesy of the Irish Architectural Archive.

p. xiv NLI, Ephemera collection, EPH F298; courtesy of the National Library of Ireland.

pp 2–3 NLI, Prints and Drawings, PD 4061 TX 6; courtesy of the National Library of Ireland.

p. 5 DCLA, Postcards and views collection, Box 2, PCV02-155; courtesy of Dublin City Library and Archive.

p. 6 NGI, Lithograph engraving, 1822, NGI.11596, Unknown artist, after T. Hammond; provenance unknown; licensed under a Creative Commons Attribution 4.0 International License: CC BY 4.0.

p. 7 NLI, Prints and Drawings, Ordnance Survey map 1847, Dublin (1 : 1056); courtesy of the National Library of Ireland.

pp 8–9 View of Lower Castle Yard, Dublin Castle, 1816, by R. Havell & Sons, after T.S. Roberts, courtesy of the Office of Public Works.

p. 10 Print from *The Graphic*, 10 April 1880; private collection, reproduced with permission.

p. 11 Cover print, *The Graphic*, 14 February 1891; private collection, reproduced with permission.

p. 13 Cover print, *Illustrated London News*, 18 April 1895; private collection, reproduced with permission.

p. 15 DCLA, Birth of the Republic collection, Postcard, BOR F51-56; courtesy of Dublin City Library and Archive.

p. 16 NLI, Hogan-Wilson collection, HOGW 152; courtesy of the National Library of Ireland.

p. 17   NAI, Department of the Taoiseach, TSCH/3/S1/2; reproduced by permission of the Director of the National Archives, Ireland.

p. 20   'Lord French in Dublin Castle', *Illustrated London News*, 18 May 1918; © Illustrated London News Ltd/Mary Evans Picture Library.

p. 21   NLI, Piaras Béaslaí collection, BEA 12; courtesy of the National Library of Ireland.

p. 25   The Military Archives, Dublin, Military Service Pensions Collection MSP34REF23407 (Annie Smith); courtesy of The Military Archives.

p. 26   NLI, Piaras Béaslaí collection, BEA 58; courtesy of the National Library of Ireland.

pp 28–9   NLI, Political Photographs, 1916–1922, NPA PHOP1; courtesy of the National Library of Ireland.

pp 30–31 British Cartoon Archive, LSE6458, cartoon by David Low, 23 November 1920; © Associated Newspapers Ltd/Solo Syndication, reproduced by permission of dmg Media Licensing.

p. 32   NLI, Michael Noyk papers, 1919–1960, MS 36,223/3/29; courtesy of the National Library of Ireland.

p. 33   NLI, Ephemera collection, EPH F343; courtesy of the National Library of Ireland.

p. 34   Mercier Press Archive, photograph, Dublin, 11 July 1921; reproduced by permission.

p. 35   Mercier Press Archive, photograph, Dublin, 11 July 1921; reproduced by permission.

pp 36–7   NLI, Prints and Drawings, Shemus Cartoon collection, PD 4398 TX 103; courtesy of the National Library of Ireland.

p. 44   NLI, Hogan-Wilson collection, HOGW 126; courtesy of the National Library of Ireland.

pp 48–9   NLI, Irish Political Scenes Folder B, photograph by J.J. Gallagher, NPA DOCD6; courtesy of the National Library of Ireland.

p. 54   NAI, Department of the Taoiseach, TSCH/1/1/1; reproduced by permission of the Director of the National Archives, Ireland.

p. 57, top   Alamy, Smith Archive/Alamy, 2BWFHHPG; reproduced courtesy of Alamy.

p. 57 bottom RTÉ Archives, Cashman Collection, 1989/001; courtesy of RTÉ Archives.

p. 58   Alamy, Smith Archive/Alamy, 2BWFHP6; reproduced courtesy of Alamy.

pp 62–3   'Rialtas Sealadach na hÉireann at the British citadel in Ireland—the surrender of Dublin Castle', *Illustrated London News*, 21 January 1922; © Illustrated London News Ltd/Mary Evans Picture Library.

p. 64   NLI, Hogan-Wilson collection, HOGW 72; courtesy of the National Library of Ireland.

p. 68   NLI, Civil War Prints photographic collection, photo by Joseph Cashman, NPA CIVP4; courtesy of the National Library of Ireland.

pp 70–71   Alamy, Smith Archive/Alamy Stock Photo, 2BWFHPT; reproduced courtesy of Alamy.

p. 72   Alamy, Smith Archive/Alamy, 2BWFHPP; reproduced courtesy of Alamy.

p. 74   NAI, Department of the Taoiseach, TSCH/1/1/1; reproduced by permission of the Director of the National Archives, Ireland.

p. 75   NAI, Department of the Taoiseach, TSCH/1/1/1; reproduced by permission of the Director of the National Archives, Ireland.

p. 77   NAI, Department of the Taoiseach, TSCH/3/S1/7; reproduced by permission of the Director of the National Archives, Ireland.

p. 79   NLI, Holloway Playbills collection, EPH E395; courtesy of the National Library of Ireland.

p. 86   Irish Capuchin Archives, IE CA IR-1/8/3/2/C, *The plain people* (*Na daoine macánta*), 16 April 1922; courtesy of the Irish Capuchin Archives.

p. 90   NLI, Irish Newspaper Archive, *Belfast News-Letter*, 17 January 1922, p. 5; courtesy of the National Library of Ireland.

pp 92–3   Alamy, Smith Archive/Alamy, 2BWFHR4; reproduced courtesy of Alamy.

pp 94–5   Alamy, Smith Archive/Alamy, 2BWFHP6; reproduced courtesy of Alamy.

p. 98   NLI, Erskine Childers papers, MS 48,084/2; courtesy of the National Library of Ireland.

p. 99   NLI, Erskine Childers papers, MS 48,068/12; courtesy of the National Library of Ireland.

p. 101   Rialtas Sealadach na hÉireann stamp overprint, 1922; private collection, reproduced with permission.

p. 103   'Palestine Gendarmerie paraded at Plymouth', *The Sphere*, 10 June 1922; © Illustrated London News Ltd/Mary Evans Picture Library.

p. 104   NLI, Ephemera collection, EPH B95; courtesy of the National Library of Ireland.

p. 106   Cairo Demonstrations 1919, Mideastimage.com; available at: commons.wikimedia.org/wiki/File:Cairo-Demonstrations1919.jpg.

p. 107   British Cartoon Archive, LSE6183, cartoon by David Low, 16 December 1919; © Associated Newspapers Ltd/Solo Syndication, reproduced by permission of dmg Media Licensing.

p. 111   Alamy, Matteo Omied/Alamy, *Indian Express*, 15 August 1947, reproduced courtesy of Alamy.

p. 114   UCD Archives, Éamon de Valera Papers, P150/3851; reproduced by kind permission of UCD-OFM partnership

pp 122–3   RTÉ Archives, Cashman Collection, 1989/010; courtesy of RTÉ Archives.

p. 126   RTÉ Archives, Cashman Collection, 0505/063; courtesy of RTÉ Archives.

pp 130–31   NAI, Department of the Taoiseach, TSCH/3/S26/1; reproduced by permission of the Director of the National Archives.

p. 133   NLI, Ephemera collection, EPH G18; courtesy of the National Library of Ireland.

p. 134   South Dublin Libraries, Local Studies collection, AD015; courtesy of South Dublin County Libraries.

p. 135   NLI, Independent Newspapers (Ireland) collection, INDH148; courtesy of the National Library of Ireland.

pp 136–7   NLI, Hogan-Wilson collection, HOGW 54; courtesy of the National Library of Ireland.

p. 139   NAI, Department of the Taoiseach, TSCH/3/S2159/1; reproduced by permission of the Director of the National Archives, Ireland.

p. 140   RTÉ Archives, Cashman Collection, 0505/068; courtesy of RTÉ Archives.

p. 142   RTÉ Archives, Cashman Collection, 0505/063; courtesy of RTÉ Archives.

pp 144–5   NLI, Independent Newspapers (Ireland) collection, INDH219D; courtesy of the National Library of Ireland.

p. 146   NAI, Department of the Taoiseach, TSCH/3/S1/1; reproduced by permission of the Director of the National Archives, Ireland.

pp 148–9   DCLA, Dublin City Library and Archive, uncatalogued; courtesy of Dublin City Library and Archive.

pp 154–5   Alamy, Engraving, Chris Hellier/Alamy, M41HDW; reproduced courtesy of Alamy.

p. 157   UCD Archives, Batt O'Connor papers, P68/4; reproduced by kind permission of UCD Archives.

pp 160–61   NLI, Independent Newspapers (Ireland) collection, INDH122; courtesy of the National Library of Ireland.

pp 170–71   Print from *Illustrated London News*, September 1893; private collection, reproduced with permission.

Acknowledgements

This book was completed during the uniquely challenging circumstance of the COVID-19 pandemic, and we would like to record our thanks to the following for the myriad ways in which they assisted with its researching, writing and publication: Valeria Cavalli, Sophie Evans, Sarah Gearty, Ruth Hegarty, Michael Kennedy, Helena King, Patrick Maume and Fidelma Slattery (Royal Irish Academy); Orlaith McBride, Niamh McDonnell, Tom Quinlan and Zoë Reid (National Archives); William Derham and John McMahon (Office of Public Works); Daniel Ayiotis (Military Archives); Kate Manning (UCD Archives); Tara Doyle, Charlotte Fabian and Brendan Teeling (Dublin City Libraries and Archives); and Rónán Whelan (Department of Tourism, Culture, Arts, Gaeltacht, Sport and Media).

We would also like to thank Nicholas Allen, Barry Houlihan, Martin Maguire, Kathryn Milligan, Deirdre McMahon, Breandán Mac Suibhne, William Murphy, Brian Ó Conchubair, Grace O'Keeffe, Hussein Omar, Darina Wade, Ciarán Wallace, and the staff of Athlone, Donaghmede, Moate and Raheny public libraries.

Previous pages: 'A view of Dublin Castle', print of a view of part of the Castle grounds, originally published in *Illustrated London News*, September 1893.

Index
-----

*Page numbers in **bold italic** refer to illustrations/photographs*